Research Methodology

A Handbook

About the Author

Born of 5th September, 1930, Professor Misra is an internationally known geographer, regional planner, and Gandhian scholar. He has numerous books on his credit on Gandhian Thought, local and regional planning, rural development urbanization, and ecology and environment. He did his Ph.D. at the University of Maryland, College Park, Maryland, USA in 1964 under the Fulbright Programme of US Government.

Professor Misra is known for his Growth Poles and Center Theory now being widely used in urban and regional development planning all over the world. Micropolitan approach to rural transformation is his other major contribution to development theory. He has written/edited over 100 books and over 150 articles on various themes published both in India and abroad. Among the positions Professor Misra has held from time to time, a few are listed below:

1. Professor, Department of Geography, Delhi School of Economics, Delhi University, Delhi (1987-95);
2. Vice Chancellor, Allahabad University, Allahabad (1984-87);
3. Vice Director and Chief Technical Advisor, United Nations Center for Regional Development (UNCRD), Nagoya, Japan (1979-84);
4. Founder Director, Institute of Development Studies, University of Mysore, Mysore (1971-1979);
5. Consultant UNDP, Teheran, Iran,1975-76; and UN Research Institute for Social Development (UNRISD), Geneva, Switzerland (1972-73).

Professor Misra can be contacted at:
35/1 Stanley Road
Allahabad -211001
Mobile: 91 9450869688
E-mail: sdf.misra@gmail.com

Research Methodology

A Handbook

Revised and Enlarged Edition

R.P. Misra

CONCEPT PUBLISHING COMPANY PVT. LTD.
NEW DELHI-110059

ISBN-13: 978-93-5125-116-3 (HB)
ISBN-13: 978-93-5125-117-0 (PB)

First Published 1989
Reprint 2001, 2002
Revised and Enlarged Edition 2016

Published and Printed by

Concept
Since 1974

Concept Publishing Company Pvt. Ltd.
Regd. Office: A/15-16, Commercial Block, Mohan Garden, New Delhi-110059 (INDIA)
Phones : 25351460, 25351794, *Fax* : 091-11-25357109
E-mail : publishing@conceptpub.com
Website: www.conceptpub.com

Editorial Office: H-13, Bali Nagar, New Delhi-110 015, India.

Misra, R. P., 1930- **author.**
Research methodology : a handbook / R.P. Misra. — Revised and enlarged edition.
pages cm
Includes bibliographical references and index.
ISBN 9789351251163 (HB)
ISBN 9789351251170 (PB)

1. Social sciences—Research—Methodology. 2. Technical writing. I. Title.

H62.M57 2016 DDC 300.72 23

Preface

This handbook on research methodology has been very popular among students pursuing their M.Phil. and Ph.D. degrees. It has also been popular among those who secure funds from various governments and other agencies for research in social sciences including geography and related disciplines. With the addition of a chapter on statistical analysis, the value of the book has further increased.

This book is a complete manual of research and I am sure that it would continue to be popular among researchers in future too. I welcome any comments on the book or its various chapters from the readers especially the research students.

I thank the Concept Publishing Company Pvt. Ltd., New Delhi for publishing the book and selling it at a price within the reach of even economically weak students and researchers.

Allahabad **R.P. Misra**

August 1, 2016

Contents

List of Tables

List of Figures

1
Introduction

Research is a process and a means to acquire knowledge about any natural or human phenomena. Rapid social, economic and technological changes of modern times are causes as well as effects of new discoveries, inventions and findings in various walks of life. It is often said that research is one of the biggest industries of modern times and it may very well consume half the GNP of the USA by the turn of this century. Even in India, it is estimated that at least 20 per cent of national income will be invested in research directly or indirectly by 2050 A.D.

Research plays two roles: (1) it contributes to the general fund of knowledge, and (2) it helps solve many complex problems of the society. Research is, therefore, often classified as pure and applied. The pure, basic or fundamental research "involves the asking and answering of questions that do not involve immediate solutions of pragmatic problems".[1] It is generated because one gets intellectually involved in it. Applied research is conducted with a view to solve a given problem—it is more directly concerned with mundane human needs—food, clothing, shelter, lifestyle, institutions, etc. Thus, while pure research advances the frontiers of knowledge, applied research uses this knowledge to solve varied social, economic, technological and other problems of the society.

The distinction between pure and applied research is,

however, not as clear-cut as it appears to be. In fact the two are interdependent and go together and often merge into a common whole. Without a body of fundamental knowledge, applied research would not be feasible. For example, the nuclear research of applied nature would not be possible without the theory of relativity. Newton's law of gravitation became the foundation for many applied researches. The reverse is also true. Many discoveries of fundamental nature have emerged incidentally or as by-products of applied research. So, the controversy over fundamental *versus* applied research is largely academic.

Such being the importance of research every effort should be made to offer adequate training facilities in research methodology. There is, however, no short-cut to learning the process of scientific research both general and specific to a particular discipline. Only when the researcher undertakes research, he learns its nuances and problems. Many of the frustrating hours, he wastes in this process can, however, be avoided or at least minimised if he has access to literature on research methodology. This handbook is designed to provide an elementary foundation in research methodology for those who have just entered the field of research in social sciences and other related disciplines.

The handbook is not meant to be an all inclusive and comprehensive work on research methodology. It attempts only to give a skeleton of the methods and procedures a researcher should know in order to optimize his research results and to be able to present his research findings in an acceptable manner and form. It does not include methods and techniques used in the analysis of data. Those interested in these aspects of research should consult other relevant publications referred to in the text.

The material for this volume has been drawn from a variety of published and unpublished sources. I do not claim any original contribution except in matters of organization and presentation. What prompted me to put these materials together in this form is the conviction that every researcher must know the basics of research procedure before he embarks on any meaningful research work. I do hope that the objectives with which the book has been written will be fulfilled and many a student would benefit from the suggestions and procedures explained in it.

Note

1. Robert W. Durrenberger, *Geographical Research and Writing,* New York, T.Y. Crowell Co., 1971, p. 3.

2

On Scientific Method

"In the beginning God created the heaven and the earth."[1] This was the beginning. Whether a person chooses to believe in the religious or the scientific origin of life, there must be agreement that somewhere, somehow, it all began. It is from this beginning that everything has evolved. So it is with science and the scientific method.

In the earliest stages of man's development, mythology was used almost entirely to explain unusual occurrences of everyday life which would otherwise have remained a mystery forever. Using myths may seem a very crude manner of explanation to interpret certain phenomenon, compared to present day thinking, but it was a significant advance from that period in history when no explanation of any kind was given. Man had thus progressed from a non-thinking animal to one who questioned the existence of things around him.

Even in those moments of early history, one can imagine a prehistoric man applying science to the eating of a plant. He no doubt approached the new plant with a problem in mind, he was hungry. *He then formed a hypothesis based on his previous empirical observations;* the plant was edible since it had the same colour or the same shape or similar appearance to other plants he had previously eaten. *Next he applied the empirical study,* he ate the plant. If he died or was violently ill, the plant was not edible and his hypothesis was rejected. If he lived and was nourished by the plant, his hypothesis was accepted and another milestone in the development of science had passed. Had another prehistoric man witnessed his death and learned from this observation that the plant was inedible, the experiment was still a success. However, if no one witnessed his death, the experiment had to be repeated until the knowledge gained could be passed on to the rest of the people.

Thus, step-by-step, using our imagination, we can visualize the evolution of science throughout prehistoric times. Many great benefits to mankind occurred during this period of history. Such developments as the use of fire, the use of weapons, the use of metal, and the use of the wheel is evidence of it. However, these great discoveries occurred very slowly, perhaps primarily by chance, indicating a need for a definite method of approach for the solution of problems. We must remember, however, that this need was not met in a day. It took considerable amount of time and experimentation and evolved through the years as science itself evolved. By examining the contributions of some people to different fields of study, we can actually visualize how their application of a precise method of thought and analysis to the solving of a problem was a major contribution to the growth of science. In addition, we can also see that as knowledge accumulated, there arose a need for specialization and the proper division of this increasing mass of knowledge into workable, manageable parts.

The first development of scientific ideas occurred in astronomy.[2] As early as 580 B.C., the Ionian philosopher, Thales of Miletus, questioned the mythological view about the movement of stars and planets. The observations and notations that the stars revolved in pattern about a central star, the North Star, was the beginning of empirical observation. About 450 B.C. such Greek philosophers and scientists as Empedcles,

Leucippus, Democristus, and later, the Roman poet and scientist, Lucretius, gave the world its foundations of atomic theory.[3] These men were experts in all the known fields of study of their time. Aristotle (384-322 B.C.)[4] made contributions to the fields of rhetoric, biology, zoology, philosophy, physics, and the arts. The division of science into manageable parts had its beginning with Aristotle:

> "Aristotle divided reality into several spheres of physics, biology, ethics, politics, and psychology; and the reality which he studied in these spheres was the observable facts."[5]

Inductive reasoning was also advanced by Aristotle. He believed in observing all things, classifying them precisely, and from this, arriving at generalizations. Euclid (*c.* 300 B.C.) at the same time added to the existing domain of science with his theories of geometry, derived from his method of reasoning: the deductive method.[6] Before their conquest by Romans, the Greeks also originated the study of mechanics and other specialized areas of science.

This growing accumulation of knowledge and the continuing conquest of the unknown by the Greeks was brought to an abrupt end during the Dark Ages of European history.[7] The conflict that raged during these Ages took a heavy toll of books, records and libraries. This continued until the eleventh century. Thereafter, the works of the Greeks were rediscovered and the examination, evaluation, and arguments over them continued through the twelfth and thirteenth centuries. The alchemists of the thirteenth and fourteenth centuries rediscovered many of the experimental procedures used by the Alexandrians in their search for a transmuter of base metal into gold.[8] However, these activities were branded as witchcraft by the society of that time and scientific advance remained halted until the fifteenth century.

The birth of present day science could be traced to Leonardo da Vinci (1452-1519), Nicholas Copernicus (1473-1543), Vesalius (1514-1564), and Galileo Galilei (1564-1642) in the period of history known as the Renaissance.[9] These independent thinkers of their time began to observe, to experiment, and to record their findings in the fields of anatomy, physics, aerodynamics, and dynamics. These men were experts in many different fields but knowledge had grown to such an extent that they could no longer, as had the early Greeks, master all the existing scientific knowledge of their world. Galilei not only contributed to science with his theory of dynamics, but his research method stands out as an achievement by itself. He analysed his problem down to its basic root, derived hypotheses to solve them, and then proceeded to prove which hypothesis was right.[10] This is the origin of today's scientific method which was not formulated into a formal method for many years to come. Sir Isaac Newtons' (1642-1727) discovery enabled the accumulation of knowledge to finally result in a major break through the barrier of the unknown.

> "...that all the movements of the heavens could be described by one simple law was the first great physical synthesis, and perhaps represents the highest achievement in the history of science."[11]

Science and the scientific method then moved forward at a rapidly increasing rate; Lavoisier (1743-1794) in the field of chemistry,[12] Charles Darwin (1809-1882) in the field of genetics and heredity,[13] Pasteur (1822-1895) in the field of bacteriology,[14] Benjamin Franklin, Thomas Jefferson, Robert Fulton, Thomas Edison, Alexander Graham Bell, Albert Einstein, and many others made major contributions. Today rapid strides are being made in all fields of science. How is this advance being accomplished? The answer lies not in science, *per se*, but in the method. How is this scientific method acquired?[15] The answer lies simply in the correct use of the methods of thought handed down by the scientists and which collectively is called the scientific method. Scientists, throughout history, contributed to evolving methods of reasoning. These methods were summarized, and argued for, by the following: Francis Bacon (1561-1626) gave us his perfected theory of induction; Rene Descartes (1596-1650), his ideal method, the theory of deduction; Morris Cohen (1880-1947), his method that the formulation of hypothesis must come first; and John Dewey (1859-1952), the concept that before anything else, there must be a successful identification of the problem.[16]

The scientific method does not use any single one of the above methods but incorporates all of them into a definite means of eventually solving any problem or phenomena of nature that may arise. As early as the sixteenth century, Galilei used this method to solve his problem of dynamics.

Scientific Method and Scientific Research

Scientific method may be defined as:

> "A collective term denoting the various processes by the aid of which the sciences are built up.[17]

More specifically, scientific method could be defined as consisting of four major parts: (1) identification of the problem, (2) formulation of an hypothesis, (3) systematically collecting, classifying, and analyzing data, and (4) either acceptance or rejection of the hypothesis. Thus, by tracing the history of science, the evolution of a method for the further advancement of science has been revealed. Here is the universal tool, handed down after years of being perfected, by which the understanding of any phenomenon in nature may be achieved.

This scientific method is applicable to any branch of science:

> "Scientific method must itself be taught. The teaching of the facts and principles alone of one or more of the particular sciences, although it may imply much of scientific method, is not enough...."[18]

The learning of the facts of a particular branch of science without learning how to derive them or other presently unknown facts is really not becoming a scientist:

> "The authors believe that of all the things which may be learned in proceeding through the various steps in formal education—particularly during the later steps — nothing is more valuable than the mastering of sound principles of methodology."[19]

There has been much incongruity among researchers as to what the scientific method consists of. Some say that there is no one method; there are different methods which have distinctive characteristics which are peculiar to the discipline of science in which they are used. It is also thought that methods may differ within a specific discipline, that is to say, they may differ from researcher to researcher. It has been said:

> "There is no such thing as the scientific method. The methods of science vary from one field of inquiry to another. They vary from one research worker to another within a field, and even from investigation to

> investigation by a single worker. It is possible, however, to find a pattern common to virtually all scientific research. This pattern consists essentially of four elements or steps: (1) the assembly of facts or existing information; (2) the formation of an hypothesis or hypotheses; that is, the formation of a system of general propositions to explain the behaviour of the facts; (3) the prediction, which is an explanation obtained by deducing from the hypothesis specific conclusions not already known from the mere collection of facts; and (4) the testing of the prediction by reference again to observed facts.[20]

It is obvious that any research or inquiry which is to yield sound, unbiased knowledge or fact must involve a method. This method allows an investigator to correlate his knowledge of facts and statistics with creative imagination to his attempt to make additions to the fund of organized knowledge in his discipline.

In studying the development of science and the scientific method, we first encounter the elements of rationalism and empiricism. The entity of rationalism lies in man's ability to discover truth through his powers of reasoning. That is to say, through reasoning, any meaningful question the mind can propound can be answered. When used as a method, rationalism is composed of two elements. These are intuition and deductive logic. The intuitive concept suggests that all metaphysical ideas or principles are innate or inborn and that the comprehension of such principles is evident to one's self. The concept of deductive logic allows one to derive theorem or to answer questions by use of intuitively known laws or axioms.

The developing of knowledge by making a great number of accurately recorded observations and experiments was not to the taste of the Greeks. They were filled with curiosity about the world in which they lived and spent much time in the discussion of abstract principles. They felt that it was degrading to tinker with the various tools, vessels and mechanical contrivances which were available to them, so they did not advance such disciplines as chemistry or physics, but were quite successful in the development of geometry where the exercising of pure reasoning was required more than observation and experimentation.

One of the major Greek contributors to the rationalistic concept of methodology was Aristotle. His concepts remained prevalent until the latter part of the Middle Ages. At this time, innovations in methodology began to occur with the onset of empiricism as an opposing philosophy. One of the last prominent philosophers to hold to this rationalist concept was Descartes. He attempted to initiate some slight changes in this concept. He felt that accepted laws and principles should be subjected to the process of doubting that those that could not stand as absolute truth should be discarded and the residual be used in deducing knowledge. Since he was a mathematician, he could doubt all those axioms except those of mathematics.

One major criticism of the rationalistic concept was that the intuitive laws or principles which were self-evident would insinuate that they would be evident to one's self and this being a personal characteristic would inject individual bias. However, if intuition can be related to imagination, it is necessary to accept it as an indispensable part of the scientific method. If imagination is lacking, it is impossible to develop hypotheses. The result of imagination or intuition can be subjected to the test of empirical research.

Francis Bacon understood the importance of a new way of investigation of nature and was the first to develop the concept of empiricism as methodology. He wrote a book called *Novum*

Organum (1620), which means *The New Instrument,* and which opposed the logical works of Aristotle called the *Organon.* He called *Organon* an "old instrument" and the empirical method as the new instrument. He believed that one should utilize inductive methodology when in pursuit of sound knowledge.

In elaboration on Bacon's methodology some thought that one should begin with facts revealed by sensual perceptions and develop axioms and finally laws. Using this concept, one can sum up the aim and method of modern science by classifying facts and forming judgements should be made independent of any mental constitution of the researcher. After this classification of facts has been made and their-relationships established, the next step is the use of creative imagination in arriving at scientific laws. From the above philosophy, one could see a possible method being implied; namely, (1) gather facts, (2) classify these facts and establish relationships, (3) use the imagination in formulating scientific law, (4) criticize and judge the soundness.

One major criticism of this methodology is that there is no implication of a problem. The classification of the innumerable facts would be impossible without some hypothesis with which to proceed. Another criticism is that the verification of facts by the use of judgement only is insufficient. It is obvious that a method is needed which will integrate both empiricism and rationalism (induction and deduction).

The modern concepts of deduction and induction tend to set the two up as opposing methodologies of science. When using deduction, a premise is developed. The concern is not with the truth or falsity of the premise, but rather what must be true if the premise is true. In induction, the concern is directed at whether the premise is true. Therefore, one can say induction is a method by which the truth of the premise or hypothesis is established.

From the considerations above, the major constituents of a scientific method were derived. The deductive analysis begins with propositions that are not accepted as self-evident. They are termed hypothesis. This does not exclude those propositions which have been tested and accepted as laws of science. Here one can observe the drifting of the deductive method away from the rationalistic one. One can observe from this that facts are used to formulate hypothesis which are then tested and verified and become facts; from these facts, more hypothesis can be developed. To simply know facts is insufficient. There must be some sort of inquiry or problem arising from the recognition of insufficient knowledge to explain the relationship of facts observed. Imagination plays an important role in the formulation of hypothesis to arrive at this explanation. Here one sees the inductive part of the method come into play in the establishment of the relation of the known facts with the hypothesis.

It is thought by some that the major contribution of John Dewey to the method of research was the emphasis which he placed on the problem area being the first thing to be considered. He thought that it was this problem area which was the impetus to the assembly of relevant facts and the subsequent development of the. hypothesis. Prior to this philosophy, those who initiated certain methodologies either completely omitted or belittled the significance of the problem area. Dewey was a moral philosopher and has no intention of contributing to a research method in science; rather his proposals were intended to answer normative questions pertaining to the resolving of tensions or difficulties in authentic situations.

Dewey's philosophy had a pragmatic concept which brought about the proper mental attitude for conducting research. This concept was that of placing the correct emphasis on the consequences of research, the facts to be gained. He thought that his philosophy was not pragmatic but experimental or instrumental. Others saw this as being related to the pragmatic meaning of truth that people had to experience before it was accepted as truth. From Dewey's philosophy, the following research method was developed:

1. *A problem area:* The lack of an explanation as to the outcome of related factual action.
2. *The formulation of a problem:* An explanation of the problem area.
3. *Hypothesis development:* Possible explanation of factual action as related to a consequence.
4. *Processing evidence:* Locating area in experience where this factual action and consequence exist.
5. *The test:* The experiment is conducted and the consequences are observed.

When comparing Dewey's method with one utilised in the directing of positive research, one finds both harmony and conflict. Positive research is concerned with the problems of a society, which is harmonious with the first step in Dewey's method. However, Dewey's tendencies toward moral philosophy lead to a difference in the last step of his method. His technique of verification entailed a proposal or a recommending of corrective action to be taken by people and if satisfactory results are obtained, i.e., hypothesis was verified.

Discrete analysis of the methods of research proposed by men such as Dewey, Francis Bacon, and others has yielded a method which would facilitate fruitful and positive research. It consists of (1) the recognition of a problem area and the searching out of the related questions which, when answered, will offer an explanation of the problem, (2) a compiling of the facts relevant to the questions which have been developed, (3) formulation of a hypothesis that is consistent with the facts previously assembled and that lends itself to a deductive analysis in which new facts may be predicted, and (4) verification: the observation of new facts which are consistent with the hypothesis.

The interpretations of the method stated above may vary from one discipline to another. However, there are certain characteristics which are consistent with all disciplines. For example, a research effort in any discipline will be rendered useless if the problem is stated in such a way that no possible answer can be found. The answer to any research problem must be accessible through the use of existing research techniques or one which can be developed. This is to say, it must be possible to formulate a hypothesis which lends itself to testing. When constructing questions to be answered by way of a research effort, one must consider the directional criteria related to obtaining answers through research and those answers which are considered acceptable. This could lead to some of the variation in the method which is observed among different disciplines.

It is erroneous for one to think that the formulation of the hypothesis comes with ease subsequent to stating the problem. This formulation is accomplished after the engagement of a creative imagination which is guided by a prior assembly of the related facts.

The verification of the hypothesis is a point of disagreement among some scientists. This may well arise from differences in the definition of the term. Some contend that the verification of a hypothesis may be obtained only if a particular course of action is followed by a segment of our society and this particular hypothesis cannot or may never be verified. Others contend that such a hypothesis is not scientific and before a hypothesis can be categorised as scientific it should be an explanation of facts and its verification will depend upon its yielding of new sound knowledge. This verification should be of a sufficient degree to alleviate any doubt in the minds of accepted authorities in that particular discipline. The statistical inference provides the necessary tools for such a verification.

The disharmony among scientists as to whether there is one scientific method or many methods results mainly from definitional differences. It is believed that once congruity is obtained as to what the aims of research are, regardless of the perspective from which it is viewed, the scientific method is a guide or pathway that, when followed with unwavering devotion, will contribute facts to any organised fund of knowledge.

Bias and Prejudice in Scientific Research

In the modern world man is constantly subjected to a vast amount of publicity, advertisement, and "cause-generated" information coming his way *via* his fellow man. In addition, each person individually is exposed to his or her own unique environment and set of social and business friends or acquaintances. It is indeed within his own unique mould that each person is forced, some of course more than others, to make rationalizations, judgements, and to form opinions. These mental processes at best, are catalyzed by the mould into which each of us is cast. Francis Bacon in his, "*Idols of the Cave*", has this to say about the subject:

> "The Idols of the Cave are the idols of the individual man."

Everyone (besides the errors common to human nature in general) has a cave or den of his own, which refracts and discolours the light of nature; owing either to his own proper and peculiar nature; or to his education and conversation with others; or to the reading of books, and the authority of those he esteems and admires, or to the differences of impressions, accordingly as they take place in a mind preoccupied and predisposed or, in a mind indifferent and settled, or the like. The spirit of man accordingly (as it is meted out to different individuals) is in fact variable and full of perturbation, and governed, as it were, by chances. It was rightly observed by Heraclitus that men look for sciences in their own lesser worlds, and not in the greater or common world.

The idols of the cave take their rise in the peculiar constitution mental or bodily, of each individual; and also in education, habit and accident. Of this kind there is a great number and variety. We instance here only those the pointing out of which contains the most important caution and which are most likely to disturb the clarity of understanding.

Men become attached to certain particular sciences and speculations, either because they fancy themselves the authors and inventors thereof, or because they have bestowed the greatest pains upon them and become most habituated to them. But men of this kind if they betake themselves to philosophy and contemplations of a general character, distort and colour them in obedience to their former predilections.[21]

It is not to be construed from the above that all those engaged in the various fields of research are influenced by these factors to the extent that their work is rendered useless. Oftentimes, the recognition of certain pitfalls and dangers in an endeavour is sufficient to cope with it. There is an element of research which we might term "creeping bias" which means that the researcher is not consciously aware that a psychological force is influencing his thinking. For example, if, in urban research, one were to attempt to ascertain the relative efficiency of a large and a small town, judgement may be influenced by one's liking or disliking for large or small towns. If the researcher in question had been closely associated with a small town in a rural setting, he may not want to show evidence that the larger town was a more economically sound unit. Although this is an oversimplified illustration, it well illustrates a weakness not always recognized in research.

As pointed out in Bacon's essay, the statement, opinions, and judgements of those whom we esteem affect in no small way, our own thinking. Oftentimes this prevents objective, original, and independent thinking and research. As researchers we need to apply the same criteria in evaluating others' thinking that we would apply to field research. In this light we have become "truly objective" although it must be recognized that objectivity is a relative term and much abused.

Personal experiences of an individual also play a very important part in the induction of bias and prejudice. If an individual has experienced on several occasions, by participation, the unprofitability of a certain agricultural enterprise, it is likely that he will rationalize his failures by generalization of such experienced unprofitability. That is, he may state, "This agricultural enterprise is unprofitable", without examining for weaknesses which, upon correction, might make the same enterprise highly profitable. Furthermore, the individual may carry his prepossessed opinion even after conditions affecting the profitability have changed markedly.

Many inductive inferences are made upon the basis of observations of data as evidence. Indirectly, at least, prejudice and bias affect the perception obtained from observation. We need to explore some of the fallacies in observation created by bias and prejudice.

Incomplete Observation

"Incomplete observation consists in overlooking or neglecting either instances or related circumstances which should be observed.[22] This is related to the previous discussion of prejudice, since the most common form of this fallacy is the selection of positive proofs or evidence and the neglect of negative proofs or instances due to bias, inattention, interest, or selective memory.

Charles Darwin recognized the importance of selective memory when he said,

> "I had also during many years, followed a golden rule—namely, whenever a published fact, a new observation or thought came across me, which was opposed to my general results, to make a memorandum of it without fail and at once, for I had found by experience that such facts and thoughts were far more apt to escape from the memory than favourable ones."[23]

People who believe themselves in possession of powers of prediction are prone to this fallacy, due to the fact they remember and record only those instances where their predictions have been fulfilled. It is for the same reason a source of superstitions, irrational belief in predictions from astrology, fortune telling, and dreams.

Inaccurate Observation

There are three types of factors—namely physical, physiological, and psychological, which are the forerunners of inaccurate observation. We are concerned here only with the psychological factors as they are related to our discussion of bias and prejudice.

The factors might include emotion, imagination, and misplaced attention all of which may result in the lack of objectiveness and the work or observation may be deemed inaccurate or biased or prejudiced although not consciously planned so.

Some of the most common or sought after evidence in research is the establishment of causes or cause and effect relationships. There are many opportunities in this quest for causes that lend themselves to the cause of the biased and prejudiced individual as well as the individual who is incompetent. Some of these are the (1) attributing cause to preceding event; that is to say that because two events occur in sequence that one is related to the other, for example, if we developed a cold after sitting next to a draft; (2) failure to eliminate irrelevancies or those factors which improperly stated affect the results; (3) establishing false relationships, for example, noting a bumper corn crop following planting during the "Upside" of the moon; (4) confusing cause and effect; for example, an individual may claim that a poverty-stricken childhood led him to crime whereas the truth may be that this background only provided the conditions favourable to crime; and (5) lack of necessary conditions: for example, a carburettor may be necessary to run an engine but it in no way is sufficient because many other items such as a starter, battery, etc., are also needed.

The presence of bias and/or prejudice in the scientific method and research is a problem that the researcher must be consciously aware of and on guard against. Bertrand Russel has said, "The kernel of the scientific outlook is the refusal to regard our own desires, tastes, and interests as affording a key to the understanding of the world". The researcher must force himself to more searching reexamination before describing his work to others who will and should judge it impartially and objectively.

Louis Pasteur gave us a good insight into this attitude when he said:

> When you believe you have found an important scientific fact and are feverishly curious to publish it, constrain yourself for days, weeks, years sometimes; fight yourself, try and ruin your own experiments, and only proclaim your discovery after having exhausted all contrary hypothesis. But when after so many efforts you have at last arrived at certainly your joy is one of the greatest that can be felt by the human soul.

Notes

1. *The Bible,* (King James Version, Cambridge Edition) London and New York: Cambridge University Press, Chapter 1, p. 1.
2. *Encyclopaedia Britannica,* Chicago. London, Toronto: Encyclopaedia Britannica Inc., 1953, Vol. 20, p. 114.
3. *Ibid.,* pp. 114-115.
4. *Ibid.,* Vol. 2, pp. 349-351.
5. *Ibid.,* pp. 352-353.
6. *Ibid.,* Vol. 20, p. 115.
7. *Ibid.,* p. 116.
8. *Ibid.,* p. 116.
9. *Ibid.,* p. 116.
10. F.S.C. Northrop, *The Logic of the Sciences and the Humanities,* New York: The MacMillan Company, 1949, p. 23.
11. *Encyclopaedia Britannica, op. cit.,* Vol. 20, p. 117.
12. *Ibid.,* Vol. 13, p. 777.
13. *Ibid.,* Vol. 7, p. 65.
14. *Ibid.,* Vol. 17, p. 358.

15. We have deliberately left out any discussion on whether science is good or bad. The eminent philosopher and scientist, Bertrand Russell states:

    "Scientific knowledge has its dangers; but so has every great thing. And over and beyond the dangers with which it threatens the present, it opens up as nothing else can the vision of a possible happy world, a world without poverty, without war, with little illness."

    See Bertrand Russell, "Science and Human Life", in *What is Science?* James R. Newman (ed.), New York: Simon and Schuster, 1955, p. 16.
16. Northrop, *op. cit.,* pp. 1-18.
17. *Encyclopaedia Britannica, op. cit.,* Vol. 20, p. 125.
18. William H. George, *The Scientist in Action–A Scientific Study of His Methods,* New York: Emerson Books, Inc., 1938, p. 326.
19. Walter Earl Spahr and Rinehart John Swenson, *Methods and Status of Scientific Research,* New York and London: Harper and Brothers, Preface p. vi.
20. Michael J. Brennan, *Preface to Econometrics,* New York: Southwestern Publishing Co., 1960, p. 2.
21. Mathew T. McClure, *The Modern Student Library,* New York: Charles Scribner's Sons, 1926, Bacon Selections, pp. 289, 295.
22. Herbert L. Searles, *Logic and Scientific Methods,* New York: Press Co. 1956, p. 320.
23. Charles Darwin, *Life and Letters of Charles Darwin,* New York: Appleton Century-Crofts, Inc. 1896, p. 71.

3

Hypothesis, Theory and Scientific Law

"Common sense" reasoning is inadequate for the depth of comprehension man requires to maintain the progress of civilization. Using "common sense" reasoning man cannot distinguish the unique or pervasive character of things. His intuition operates in terms of abstractions, which are familiar and often confused and are inadequate to express the complex structure of things.[1]

Scientific reasoning is an activity directed toward the discovery of the relationships between things or the properties of things. Using such knowledge apprehended in sensation or the imagination, man can methodologically disclose the invariant nature of particular relationships and use this new knowledge and method to extend into unknown areas and accumulate still more knowledge.[2]

Science, as stated earlier, consists of two phenomena: "a body sense" reasoning; attempting to be more intensive in approach, more vigorous in method, more accurate in conclusions, and more consequential in results.

Science may be thought of as two interrelated concepts: (1) a body of knowledge; and (2) a method of inquiry. As a body of knowledge, science contains and maintains a great quantity of laws, facts, hypotheses and theories held by transcribed account, cultural practice or individual thought. As a method of inquiry, science is concerned with the process that generates or adds to this body of knowledge.

Scientific research is the activity of using a method of inquiry to add to this body of knowledge.

> Scientific research is an... honest, exhaustive, intelligent... search for the facts, the true actualities, and their unprejudiced analysis... (to find)... their meaning or implications with reference to a given problem. Research is a state of mind—a friendly, welcoming attitude toward change. It is the problem-solving mind as contrasted to the let-well-enough-alone mind. It is the composer mind, instead of the fiddler mind; it is the tomorrow mind, instead of the yesterday mind.[3]

Scientific research is more than fact-finding, census taking, or mere taking of records. It is purposeful fact gathering, data analysis, and dynamic interpretation.

As a method of inquiry science utilizes laws, facts, hypotheses and theories to generate additional laws, facts, hypotheses and theories. This seemingly tautological statement can be readily explained when the relationships between these four concepts are clarified.

Scientists have recognized that all scientific knowledge is based on certain universal relationships between things. These unique relationships are called laws. A scientific law must be universal in concept, universal in scope and universal in quantification; that is, capable of being conceived by all people, existing in all time and all places, and involving measurable units.[4]

The relationship that is explained by laws is stated with facts. Facts are instances of laws; that is, laws are general explanations of the relationships between facts. The more general a statement, the more law-like it is; the more particular a statement, the more fact-like it is. Laws and facts are the more substantiated types of scientific knowledge. Laws are "generally accepted"[5] statements of order or relation of facts that are invariable under the stated conditions so far as it was known when the law was stated. Facts are prepositions that can be verified.[6]

Hypotheses and theories are the mechanism and the container of knowledge moving from the unknown to the known. These elements of the body and method of knowledge form the technique and the testing ground for scientific discovery.

Hypotheses (statements which assert or deny something) are adapted tentatively to explain certain facts (or relationships between facts) and to guide in the investigation of others. Hypotheses are propositions which have not been verified.[7]

Theories are more elaborate systems of hypotheses made only as the result of a great amount of investigation and thought. This system of statements, organized in a characteristic manner, is designed to serve as a partial premise for explaining as well as predicting certain types of phenomena. Theories are more substantiated propositions usually taking on a more complex structure and implying a greater range of evidence, a greater likelihood of truth, and a greater explanation of consequences.[8]

How do the laws, facts, hypotheses and theories reveal and maintain continuous revelation of more laws, facts, hypotheses and theories? How does the scientific mind move from the unknown to the known?

From the existing or supposed body of knowledge, the scientist[9] extracts certain elements (laws, facts, hypotheses and/or theories) for examination. From these elements, certain hypotheses may be made. These extensions of knowledge usually are projected toward the unknown; that is, toward an expansion of the known.

The first process of analysis usually generates a chain reaction of other processes or events. The hypotheses may be supported, attacked, added to, subtracted or restated, disproved in part or whole, disregarded, discarded, or perhaps stand for further examination. With the collection of further evidence, the acceptance and use by more people, and the combination with related knowledge, the hypotheses may achieve accepted incorporation in a theory.

The construction, testing and verification of theory is an important part of the scientific reasoning process. Standing before the jury of scientific examiners, the theory must prove its value as a carrier of truth, a servant of the mind, and a friend of the seekers of knowledge. Paul Samuelson, a contemporary American economist, made a very lucid comment on the purpose, construction and function of theory:

> Experience suggests that nature displays a mysterious simplicity if only we can discern it. This is a bonus and need not have been so. And, unrealistic, abstract models often prove useful in the hunt for these regularities… Such abstract models are like scaffolding used to build a structure; the structure must stand by itself. If the abstract models contain empirical falsities, we must jettison the models, not gloss over these inadequacies…[10]

Theories form the testing ground for the formation of laws. Utilization of theory in the conduct of further research is a form of testing in addition to providing a means for guiding the pursuit of knowledge. A theory may lack the qualities of universality and still be well formulated and quite useful as a research guide. The formation of laws is not the only means of fact finding. The utilization and testing of theory may add more facts to the field of knowledge than would be realized if the theory were accepted as a law.

Hypothesis: Development and Structure

The word hypothesis in science generally refers to a definite interpretation of a given set of facts, which is put forth as a tentative suggestion and remains partly or wholly unverified. After it is once established, it ceases to be a hypothesis and becomes a theory or explanatory principle.[11]

The word hypothesis was derived from the Greek, *hypo* (under) and *tithenas* (to place) and suggests that when the hypothesis is placed under the evidence as a foundation they tend to support one another. It performs this function by providing a proposed explanation which will have certain consequences, then may be confirmed or refuted by testing.[12]

Webster defines hypothesis as "a tentative theory of supposition provisionally adopted to explain certain facts and to guide in the investigation of others".[13] Synonyms are given as: assumption, supposition.

Nearly every great explanatory theory now accepted as valid in science was first advanced as a hypothesis. Hypotheses are suggested by the knowledge of the field already possessed by the scientist. The more thorough and extensive the knowledge of the field, the more likely the hypothesis is to be adequate to explain the facts. Imagination and scientific genius are also essential in a high degree.

Conditions for Hypothesis

There are a number of formal conditions for hypothesis. First of these is that it must be so made that deduction can be made and, consequently, a decision reached as to whether or not it does explain the facts considered. John Mill stated one condition of a genuinely scientific hypothesis: that is, it "be of such a nature as to be either proved or disproved by comparison with observed facts".[14] This is an ideal, because it is not always possible to know in advance whether a hypothesis can be confirmed or refuted.

Secondly, it should provide the answer to the problem which generated the inquiry. This does not mean to imply that all false hypotheses add nothing to research. A false hypothesis may direct attention to unsuspected facts or relations between facts. The ancient Babylonians ascribed magical powers to number 7; and in their belief that the heavenly bodies that move among the fixed stars had to be seven in number, they were led to look for and found the rarely seen planet Mercury.[15] The English logician De Morgan remarked, "Wrong hypotheses, rightly worked, have produced more useful results than unguided observation".[16]

Thirdly, a hypothesis should provide facts (from observation or test) which would reveal certain propositions to be true whose truths are not known at the time. Galileo's theory of acceleration enabled him not only to account for what he already knew when he formulated it, but also to predict that observation would reveal certain propositions to be true whose truths were not even suspected at the time. He was able to show, for example, that if the acceleration of a freely falling body was constant, then the path of projectiles fired from a gun inclined to the horizon would have to be a parabola.[17]

Fourth, it must help eliminate irrelevant facts and be simple. The simplest hypothesis that will account for the facts should be chosen.[18] Simplicity should not be confused with familiarity. To the untutored person the theory that the earth is flat is simpler than the theory that it is round. It is difficult to conceive of people at the antipodes walking on the surface of the earth without falling off. One hypothesis is said to be simpler than another if the number of independent types of elements in the first is smaller than in the second.[19]

Plane geometry is said to be simpler than solid geometry, because figures in three independent dimensions are studied in the latter and only two in the former. Unless all the assumptions of an hypothesis are explicitly stated together with the relations between them, it is difficult to say whether it is in fact simpler than another hypothesis.

A hypothesis that has an orderly system or arrangement, "simplicity of system"[20] or generality is more readily acceptable than one whose assumptions are unconnected.

Sources of Hypothesis

In order for a hypothesis to originate, some problem must exist to cause someone to start looking for facts connected with this problem. These facts are then organized. The problem cannot even be stated unless we are familiar with the subject matter in which we discover the problem.

The Greeks found a problem in the behaviour of the Nile River, because they were acquainted with the behaviour of other rivers and these rivers did not behave as did the Nile. Certain facts, such as wind, rain, snow and evaporation, were known to affect these rivers, therefore, these facts were studied in order to attempt an understanding of the Nile.[21]

To state some obscurely felt difficulty in the form of a determinate problem, we must be able to pick out, on the basis of previous knowledge, certain elements in the subject matter as significant. Thus, in his studies of the Nile, Herodotus noted the distance covered by the overflowing waters, the time this overflow began, when it reached its maximum, and the absence of breeze on the river's surface. It was in terms of such distinguishable and repeatable elements that Herodotus stated his difficulty. It was his familiarity with the behaviour of rivers which drew his attention to these elements.

In order to take a step forward in any inquiry, we begin with a suggested explanation or solution of the difficulty. When formulated as propositions, these explanations are called hypothesis. A hypothesis is believed to be relevant to a problem if it expresses determinate modes of connection between a set of facts, including the fact investigated.

Sometimes scientists see a connection between data, and then formulate a hypothesis. More often many years of hard work and disciplined research and study result in the formulation of a hypothesis.

Method of Hypothesis Formulation

The method of hypothesis is restricted to the formulation of good working suggestions and good tentative principles of explanation. It is the procedure including the rules used in reaching a hypothesis.

Certain general requirements or rules to be followed in reaching a hypothesis are usually given by logicians. They are as follows:

1. The hypothesis should be conceivable and not absurd. In other words, it must be capable of being brought into the accepted body of knowledge. Not all people must accept it; but the test of the conceivability of the hypothesis must be determined by its ability to explain the fact. Even though a hypothesis may seem absurd, it may grow into the system.

2. The hypothesis must be of such a character that deductions can be made from it.

   A hypothesis is valueless if it is not stated in such a way that various deductions can be made from it.

   The deductive elaboration of a hypothesis must follow its formation.

   Going back to the Nile, we can restate part of Herodotus' argument:

   - If hot winds blow from a region, then that region itself is hot. (*general rule*)
   - Hot winds blow from the interior of Africa. (*observed fact*)
   - The interior of Africa is hot. (*inferred fact*)
   - If snow falls in a region, then that region cannot have a hot climate. (*rule*)
   - The interior of Africa is hot. (*inferred fact from the previous inference*)
   - Snow does not fall in the interior of Africa. (*inferred fact*)

   The previous was a means of rejecting a theory that melting snows in Africa caused the Nile to inundate periodically.[22]

   In a deductive procedure, we start with certain assumed general principles and see what we can get out of them. Such assumed principles are ordinarily called postulates or axioms. Thus, for every deductive system there is a definite set of postulates or axioms on which the system as a whole is based.

   Induction is not the reverse of deduction; the two are supplementary. Every inductive inquiry starts with concrete facts and seeks to discover and formulate a general principle or law to interpret these facts.

3. A hypothesis should not contradict any of the known and proven laws.

Here again care must be taken not to throw out a hypothesis which appears to contradict these laws. A new hypothesis is likely to appear contradictory to old established laws merely because of its strangeness.

The most important element in the method of hypothesis still remains unmentioned. It is known as the process of "moulding the hypothesis". This involves two things. In the first place a good hypothesis is usually the product of a number of relatively vague guesses fused together by a process of elimination of the irrelevant ideas, and a reconstruction of what are left into a clear and definite hypothesis. In the second place, the hypothesis must also be shaped to fit the facts. By moulding is meant the process of fusing vague and indefinite ideas into the clear and precise principles of explanation, formulated so as to fit the facts under consideration and relevant to the problem. It must be emphasized that even though the hypothesis has been moulded to fit the facts it is not verified. It only becomes a working hypothesis to be established possibly by further investigation.

Method of Explanation

To effect a complete explanation of a phenomenon, it is necessary to carry on the investigation until the hypothesis is fully verified. Four stages may be distinguished in the complete method.[23]

1. Collecting the data. Given a certain problem, the first

step is to get sufficient facts, establish counting and sampling procedures and assemble or properly arrange the material.

2. The Formulation of Hypothesis.
3. Deductions from the Hypothesis.
4. Verification of the separate deductions.

There are two types of verification:

(a) Positive or to confirm;

(b) Negative or to refute.

The above four points have been discussed earlier and will not be interpreted here in detail.

Testing a hypothesis is really not a part of its development. However, a brief outline of ways of testing a hypothesis follows and may be valuable to a better understanding of its development.

1. Observation and Experimentation.
2. Mathematical Calculation.
3. Statistical Verification.
4. Verification by Elimination.
5. Verification by Disjunctive Reasoning.

In conclusion we can say that a hypothesis is an application of the old saying "Use your head to save your heels". If you were to lose your fountain pen you might search without any plan every inch of the house; but by forming hypothesis as to its possible whereabouts on the basis of where you last remembered using it, who else may have it, and eliminate these one at a time until a satisfactory one is found.[24]

The Theory and its Structure

Identification of a Theory

Henri Poincare (1854-1912), a French mathematician and philosopher of science, provided an excellent guide for the identification and understanding of the role of theory in scientific research when he said: "Science is built with facts as a house is built with stones, but a collection of facts is no more science than a heap of stones a house".[25]

Compare Poincare's reasoning with Samuelson's statement. Samuelson develops his idea more precisely in a formal definition: a theory is... "a set of axioms, postulates, or hypotheses that stipulate something about observable reality".[26]

Poincare and Samuelson imply or recognize that theory provides an organized substantiated plan of reasoning about phenomena and their interrelationships. Theory provides a systematic method for conducting scientific research and cultivates the scientific mind toward fertile areas of knowledge discovery. We would elaborate this benchmark position in the ensuing discussion.

Elements of a Theory

The structure of a theory consists of certain elements that, built one upon the other, form a deductive system of reasoning. These elements are: (1) assumptions; (2) theoretical terms, and (3) theorems.

The assumptions of a theory form a logical skeleton for the explanatory system and define the basic notions about the system.[27] Such a conceptual world or abstract model is simpler than the real world and contains only the forces that the theory asserts to be important.[28]

Theoretical terms signify either various entities that cannot be specified except by way of some theory which postulates their existence, or certain ideal limits of a theoretically endless process. As coordinators of the variables or entities in the theory to observable traits of things, these terms may be thought of as a set of rules that define the class of phenomena for which the model can be taken to be an adequate representation of the real world.[29]

Theorems should be logically deducible from the statements in the assumptions. An interpretation or model for the abstract assumptions supplies some flesh for the skeletal structure in terms of more or less familiar, conceptual, or visualizable materials.[30]

Classification of Theory

General Classifications of Theory: There has been some interest in classifying theories according to their extent of application.[31] Invariably, such separations involve two classes—pure and practical. Pure theory is considered to be logical deduction from assumed premises. Relying on intellectual speculation, pure theory builds a conceptual model for explaining observable phenomena. Practical theory, eschewing all reference to deductive reasoning, generalizes relations abstracted from observable phenomena. Practical theory is thought to put meaning and purpose into the logic of pure theory for the solution of practical problems.[32]

Independent Theories: A more precise categorization of the types of independent theory and systems of interdependent theories is given by Henryk Mehlberg, a contemporary Canadian philosopher.

An axiomatizable theory consists of all the logical consequences of a specified set of assumptions and can be deduced from a subset of such consequences, since all the assumptions are their own consequences and belong themselves to a theory. Axiomatizing a theory amounts to constructing an axiomatic system whose assumptions, theoretical terms, and theorems add up to this theory.[33]

Phenomenological theories have all their statements, both the assumptions and the consequences, about observable phenomena. Fact-like and law-like consequences must be susceptible of validation. Since the assumptions of these theories can be validated, such assumptions reduce to facts or laws and do not, therefore, enlarge the cognitive potentialities of science.[34]

Transcendent theories, as opposed to phenomenological theories, contain fact-like or law-like consequences which cannot be validated. If these theories are justifiable, they have to be included within the context of a theory system and the theory thus becomes indispensable and cannot be replaced by any combination of fact-like statements.[35]

Interdependent Theories: For historical reasons and/or to facilitate the division of scientific labour, ramified systems of theories are clustered in a single discipline, or a special science. Through inference or definition, one theory may be dependent on the other or a whole hierarchy of theory may be constructed. This interdependence is usually reciprocal.[36]

Self-correcting systems of theories are sequences of theories in which each theory presupposes, extends, and refutes its predecessor. This steady advance towards new theories which replace their predecessors seems to constitute the fundamental pattern of scientific progress.[37]

Functions of Theory

Theory has the particular functions of defining, systematizing, explaining, and predicting the relationships between phenomena. Due to overlapping functional processes, the particular functions of theory can best be understood by inclusion within two broad general functions; that is, as a language or as a body of substantive hypotheses.

As a language, theory is designed to promote *systematic* and organized methods of reasoning. Having no substantive content, it is a set of tautologies. In this role theory could be compared to a filing system where its relationships between things could be easily seen.[38]

As a body of substantive hypotheses, theory abstracts features of complex reality to *explain, predict,* and *validate* relationships between things. The hypothesis is judged by its ability to fulfil these functions for a given class of phenomena.[39]

Scientific Laws and Principles

A scientific law is a statement of universal relationships between classes, events, or facts.

> In its scientific sense the word "law" means nothing more than a regularity or uniformity in the character or relation of certain classes of facts or events. It denotes just some intrinsic character, or mode of behaviour, in certain classes of phenomena—nothing imposed on them from outside, but just an orderliness of their own nature.[40]

The term scientific law is often used ambiguously, sometimes for the principle and sometimes for the formula or statement of the principle or the phenomenon. The statement of scientific law in a simple form is an abbreviation and simplification of experience of research that establishes a scientific law. Often some accuracy is sacrificed for the sake of simplicity.

Scientific laws are generalized from facts obtained in observation, from other laws, and by logical processes. The validity of the generalizations rests on the assumption that laws of science as discovered by observing nature are uniform. In other words, if the phenomenon is observable in repetitive situations, the phenomenon may be subscribed to other similar situations where it is not directly observed.

Some philosophers, who are labelled conventionalists, state that every definition of natural law is an arbitrary stipulation, therefore, a convention. One example of an extreme conventionalist was Sir Arthur Eddington, a British philosopher. He considered an entire class of natural laws (all except the statistical ones) as mere definitions.

The difference between a stipulation and real proposition is the fact that the validity of a convention is of our own making. Natural laws can be refuted or confirmed on facts and, therefore, not a definition. A definition can be maintained under any circumstances. The observable phenomena of natural laws remain the same even if the definitions or symbols are changed.[41]

Scientists have concluded from experience that some order exists in nature, even though order or predictability does not seem perfect. In other words, the laws of nature do not seem to be rigid, but are somewhat elastic. However, actual relationships in nature may be somewhat more rigid than presently thought, because perhaps these seemingly elastic laws are affected by some undiscovered variable not understood and measurable.

If no order existed at all in nature, all conceivable and also unconceivable phenomena would be observed. Experience shows that certain events do occur and others do not. Scientists have been able to predict sequences of events, describe attributes, and express relationships. These laws have excluded certain phenomenon.

Wolf states:

> It is possible that order in nature is itself the result of evolution, that in the remote past there may have been even less order than there is now, perhaps no order at all, and that some future time nature will exhibit more order than it does now.[42]

In this statement, Wolf must be referring to uniformity in the course of nature, and not to order as expressed in laws of nature. To some, it is inconceivable that law should evolve or progress. In Darwin's *The Origin of Species,* he states his principle of survival of the fittest. This principle acting in nature brings progress, but the principle remains the same.

Indications that order could arise from disorder without the directional guidance of laws seems unlikely. Perhaps this reflects a long-held basic belief that the present state has evolved under laws resulting from a directional force in the universe. Perhaps previous disorder is really only lack of knowledge or less than full understanding as to the basic processes of the universe.

Fry has the following statement on social law:

> It is often taken for granted that the ultimate purpose of social research is to arrive at generalizations or laws. In reality, many types of research are merely attempts to get specific answers to specific questions— not to arrive at rules or generalizations.[43]

Social laws are also referred to as being much less rigid than laws of physical science. This results from the effects of the immeasurable factors of personal attitudes which do not appear to be consistent, measurable, or predictable. Attempts have been made to measure attitudes; but since they are changeable rather than fixed, it is difficult to make generalizations about attitudes. Experiments in social sciences involve the difficulty of controlling variables, especially human factors. In physical research, it is possible to better control variables and reduce their effect; but in the social sciences, the residual factors to be tested often contain important other variables that reduce the measurability of the tested factor.

An empirical law is one which is established by observation or experimentation, but there is a hesitation to assign to it the significance of natural law. Being classed a natural law gives it status of being generally applied to all cases; but due to a lack of understanding that leads to a full theoretical framework, the applications are reserved for those cases where it is specifically known to apply. Later experimentation and knowledge may shed additional light and with a greater understanding the empirical law may become a natural law.

An ultimate, primary, or basic law is one which is not deduced from another law, but stands on its own. The law of gravitation is considered to be an ultimate law. According to Westaway:

> A derivative law does not depend solely on the ultimate laws and an ultimate fact; namely, the mode of coexistence or joint action of some of the component elements of the universe.[44]

Causal laws are sometimes referred to as causal connections, conditions, or relations rather than as a specific group of laws. If cause and effect is not established, it becomes a lower order condition of coexistence. All coexistence requires is that the presence of one enables us to infer the presence of the other. A regular sequence of events does not assure a causal relationship. Causal relationship results when the causal condition triggers, enters into, or becomes a part of the effect.

Scientific laws are most often formulated from the facts that are observed in nature. In order to get meaning from a mass of facts and to more closely observe the specific phenomena, experimental techniques have been devised. These facts are classified and calibrated in order to arrive at summation of information in an attempt to test our hypothesis.

A hypothesis is a mentally constructed model which accounts for the facts. In order for a hypothesis to hold true, Braithwaite states:

> The condition for established hypothesis being law like (i.e., being, if true, a natural law) will then be that the hypothesis either occurs in an established scientific deductive system as a higher-level hypothesis containing theoretical concepts or that it occurs in an established scientific deductive system as a deductive from higher level hypotheses which are supported by empirical evidence which is not direct evidence for itself.[45]

A hypothesis may cease to be a hypothesis and become a law by the presentation of empirical evidence that facts support the statement. Often an experiment or observation must be repeated many times to ensure that it may be broadly applied as a principle or law.

Scientific laws are sometimes deduced from primary laws. For instance, Kepler's three laws are derived from the laws of gravitation and explain the orbits of the planets around the Sun.

Sometimes a comprehensive law is called a theory. A theory has less empirical evidence to reinforce it, so it is partially speculation. Theories usually draw upon accepted laws of a lower order and of comprehensive nature. Therefore, theories are farther removed from the observed facts. Theories are closer to empirical evidence than untested hypotheses.

Scientific laws become established when a majority of scientists in the field accept the explanation as best possible to explain the result of sound empirical evidence. Scientific laws may need correction after a time in the light of new knowledge. The correction may be in the form of adjusting, modifying, extending, or may be completely rejected.

The fact that law proves to be incorrect in a few cases does not affect its application to other cases where it is applicable. The law may have been the best statement possible at that time, given only the evidence available; but in the light of new information, the statement may need rejecting.[46] This does not mean that the actual phenomenon did not exist, but merely that it was incorrectly described. Scientists do not invent scientific laws, but only seek to discover and describe laws as they actually exist in nature.

The principle of Occum's razors states that when two or more theories give seemingly adequate explanation of observable phenomenon, the one which makes the fewer assumptions or the less complicated theory is preferred. J.R. Hicks uses this principle to argue for his theoretical framework of indifference curves in preference to Alfred Marshall's theory of utility in explanation of consumer choice.

In reading selections on scientific research written prior to the 1930s, it seems a most cautious approach was indicated towards broad interpretation of scientific laws and explanation. With increased knowledge being added to all fields of science in the atomic age, perhaps there has been some tendency to accept too quickly and to generalize too much in respect to new scientific laws. New discoveries need careful scrutiny before acceptance. Also, one should be careful not to generalize discoveries beyond the limits justified. These criticisms should be most carefully applied in the field of the social sciences.

Notes

1. Morris R. Cohen and Ernest Nagel, *An Introduction to Logic and Scientific Method,* New York: Harcourt, Brace and World, Inc., 1934, pp. 396-97.
2. Charles H. Kaiser, *An Essay on Method,* New Brunswick, N.J.: Rutgers University Press, 1952, pp. 77-78.
3. Frederick L. Whitney, *The Elements of Research,* New York: Prentice-Hall, Inc., 1950, pp. 20-21.
4. Henryk Mehlberg, *The Reach of Science,* Toronto University of Toronto Press, 1958, Chapter 2.
5. "Generally accepted" is a somewhat obscure term implying recognition by the authorities in the field of its application.
6. Russell L. Ackoff, *Scientific Method,* New York: John Wiley & Sons, Inc., 1962. p. 21.
7. Guy B. Brown, *Science, Its Method and Its Philosophy,* London: George Allen and Unwin, Ltd., 1950, pp. 42-43.
8. *Ibid.*
9. *Ibid.*
10. Paul A. Samuelson, "Discussion—Problems of Methodology," — *American Economic Review,* 53 (May, 1963), p. 236.
11. Daniel Dommer Robinson, *The Principles of Reasoning,* New York: D. Appleton Century Company Incorporated, 1936, p. 307.
12. Searles, *op. cit.*
13. *Websters Collegiate Dictionary,* 5th ed., Mass: G&C Merriam Company 1947, p. 491.
14. Searles, *op. cit.*

15. Morris R. Cohen, and Ernest Nagel, *An Introduction to Logic and Scientific Method,* New York: Harcourt, Brace & Company, 1934, p. 208.
16. *Ibid.,* p. 208.
17. *Ibid.*
18. Robinson, *op. cit.*
19. Cohen and Nagel, *op. cit.*
20. *Ibid.,* p. 214.
21. *Ibid.*
22. *Ibid.*
23. Robinson, *op. cit.*
24. Searles, *op. cit.*
25. Charles L. Fry, *The Technique of Social Investigation,* New York: Harper & Bros., 1934, p. 160.
26. Samuelson, *op. cit.,* p. 233.
27. Ernest Nagel, *The Structure of Science,* New York: Harcourt, Brace and World, Inc., 1961, p. 90.
28. Milton Friedman, *Essays in Positive Economics,* Chicago: The University of Chicago Press, 1953, p. 24.
29. Nagel, "Assumptions in Economic Theory," in *the Structure of Science, op. cit.*, pp. 212-213.
30. Nagel, *op. cit.*, p. 90.
31. Representative of such classification methods are the English physicist William J.M. Rankine (1820-1872) and the contemporary American agricultural economist, Bushrod Allin.
32. Cohen and Nagel, *op. cit.,* pp. 397-398; and Bushrod W. Allin, "Theory: Definition and Purpose", *Journal of Farm Economics,* 31 (August, 1949), pp. 410-16.
33. Mehlberg, *op. cit.,* pp. 205-206.
34. *Ibid.,* pp. 207-208.
35. *Ibid.*
36. *Ibid.,* pp. 208-212.
37. *Ibid.,* p. 212.

38. Friedman, *op. cit.,* p. 7, and Mehlberg, *op. cit.,* part 2, chapter 3.
39. Friedman, *op. cit.,* pp. 7-9, and Mehlberg, *op. cit.,* part 2, chapter 3.
40. A. Wolf, *Essentials of Scientific Method,* N.Y.: MacMillan Co., 1925, p. 103.
41. Herbert Feigl, and May Brodbeck, (Editors), *Reading in the Philosophy of Science,* New York, Appleton-Century-Crofts, Inc., 1953, p. 181.
42. Wolf, *op. cit.*
43. C.L. Fry, *The Techniques of Social Investigation,* N.Y.: Hayer & Brothers, 1934, p. 173.
44. F.W. Westaway, *Scientific Method,* New York: Hillman-Curl, Inc. 1937, p. 236.
45. R.B. Braithwaite, *Scientific Explanation: A Study of the Function of Theory, Probability and Law in Science,* Cambridge, Eng: University Press, 1953, p. 301.
46. A.D. Ritchie, *Scientific Method,* Paterson, N.J.: Littlefield, Adams. 1960, p. 53.

4

Design of Experiment

The purpose of an experiment is to test some suggested truth or to demonstrate some known truth. First, one or more hypothesis must be formulated. Second, one or more deduction must be drawn from these hypotheses. Third, these deductions must be tested by one or more experiment. The design of experiment will be governed by the nature of research.

The experiment is considered a way of organising the collection of evidence so as to permit one to make inferences about the tenability of a hypothesis. The hypothesis asserts that two variables have some systematic relationship to each other under a given condition. A test is made to see if either variable occurs without the other. Changes in one must be accompanied by changes in the other. They may vary in a predictable way. If either of these statements is not true, the inference of the hypothesis is considered false; otherwise it is accepted.

Any controlled experiment designed to test a hypothesis of causal relationship between a particular factor and a particular phenomenon has the following essential elements (1) Two situations (experimental and control groups) are observed which are identical in all relevant respects or whose difference is known; (2) The factor assumed to be causal if found or introduced into the experimental situation and is absent or is withheld from the control group; and (3) The presence or absence of predicted phenomenon is observed in both the experimental and the control groups.[1] The experimenter is subject to the canon of difference to the experimental group and the canon of agreement to the control group.

The "after only" experiment. The experimental and control groups are selected before the introduction of the experimental variable. The variable is introduced at a specified time and in a specified manner known to the experimenter. The groups are observed after the experimental group has been exposed to the variable. There are uncontrolled elements to which both groups are exposed. When the essential elements of the experiment are achieved, an hypothesis can be determined tenable by comparing the extent of the occurrence of the phenomenon in both groups. It is assumed that both groups were identical in all relevant respects. This condition is hard to meet in the social sciences which account for failure in "after-only" experiment. Differences between the control and experimental are due to (1) initial differences between the two groups or (2) differences in predisposition to react to or to change in relation to the experimental variable or other factors.[2]

The "before-after" experiment has the same individual as both the control and the experimental groups. The group is observed prior to its exposure to the experimental variable. The experimental factor is introduced and the group is observed again. This tends to overcome the problems of equating groups. The simulated before-after has two equated groups or samples. They are selected in advance. One group is observed before exposure to the experimental variable (the control group). The experimental group is observed after exposure. The difference between the "before" is the measure of the control group and the "after" is the measure of the experimental group is assumed to be the measure of effect of the experimental factor. This study has the same limitation as the "after-only" experiment.

Advantages and disadvantages of "after-only" and "before-after" are as follows. The respondents feel that they should give good result. The measuring process becomes distorted because of this attitude or it may exhaust the goodwill of respondents. The "after" measurement may introduce other problems, the respondent becomes bored and unwilling to respond or may give responses similar to the previous response. The after-only is not subject to the above problems. This occurs where repeated measurements are introduced.

In social experiments which run over a period of time, there is a possibility that unplanned events will affect the experimental outcome. Ways to eliminate unplanned events should be designed in the experiments. Neither design allows for changes in events over time.

The "before-after" design permits a more thorough analysis of the process of change than the "after-only" design. The before-after permits identification of individual initial characteristics, individuals with different responses, etc. Causal inferences are not based on comparison of individuals who differ in after-only experiments. "After-only" design represents the effect of experimental fact. The causal analysis in an "after-only" is limited to such factors as age, sex, religion, income, and education. The "before-after" design, given the same number of subjects, is usually more reliable than the "after-only" design.

The comparative experiment is designed to answer certain questions, precisely, formulativeness of different methods.[3] The previous experimental design can be used in a comparative effectiveness of a method used. Each method is designed to answer various questions under consideration. It is possible to dispense with control groups. The contrasting groups are considered to be the control groups.

Let us take a brief look at the methods of equating the experimental and control groups. Method under consideration will be matching controls, randomization, precision control, frequency distribution controls and variance.

The matching of controls should be used with caution. First is the careful matching of specimens to form a subject control pair as nearly alike in all pertinent features as possible. The efficiency and sensitivity of the experiment depend on the success of matching. Experimenters do not know in many cases all features which are pertinent; so judgement must exist in this design. Bias must be avoided. Most other experiments of this design are small. Far-reaching conclusions have been drawn from experiments of this nature. This is equivalent to tossing a coin. The chance of error is great.[4]

R.A. Fisher states, no matter how carefully we attempt to match conditions between two situations, the equation is necessarily incomplete and more or less defective. The answer to achieving equivalence of groups is to randomize. Random assignment of individual to experimental and control groups requires the use of procedures which give each individual an equal chance of being assigned to any given group. Individuals are numbered and a table of random numbers is used or some other method of random selection. Any difference in the group is due to chance.

Precision control is a very difficult procedure for several reasons: (1) Matching of individuals requires a large group to select from and to avoid shrinkage of sample, (2) Factors relevant to the problem are not known in all cases, (3) It is difficult to obtain adequate measures of the factors on which it may be important to match. Matching may result in error in conclusion if relevant factors which are not equalized are not randomized in two groups.

Successful matching increases efficiency by decreasing size of difference between control and experimental groups by chance alone. Groups should be matched rather than individual with individual if groups are the object of study.[5]

Frequency distribution control is an attempt to match without losing as many cases as one does in precision control. This method matches an experimental and control group in terms of overall of known factor or factors within two groups. Factors may be equated and the group can be mismatched. It may be an error to assume that the distribution of two groups is similar if averages are similar. If two distributions are equivalent, they could be drawn from the same population by chance.

In the experimental designs it is possible to achieve a matching of the groups through an analysis of covariance.[6]

The analysis of variance permits a study of complex interrelationships which is not possible by simpler designs. It permits more reliable conclusions about more hypotheses with fewer cases than if hypotheses were tested in separate design.

Randomization can prevent human bias from entering the selection of sample, assigning subjects and controls. The experimenter is ever present with the danger of psychological distortion.

Bias in the subject has posed many problems in formulating experiments. The identity of the subject and control group is cancelled from the participants, however, both groups show indications of psychological effect which cancel the effects of the exposure.

The experimenter and the subjects are influenced by psychological factors. In some cases it is possible to cancel the subjects and control groups from both the experimenter, subject and control groups. This may eliminate to a degree of bias among all concerned.

Subconscious signalling has posed some problems. The subjects or the control groups may become aware of the experimenter-grouping techniques and distort the findings. The experimenter is not aware of this signalling.

The design used by experimenters requires careful selection—two or more designs are used in one experiment. The formulation of one or more hypotheses are required for experimental research. The areas in which sufficient research is made provide excellent basis for developing hypotheses.

The types of controls vary with the purpose and questions under consideration. The "before-after" design provides a better basis for reaching conclusions when two separate groups are used. The random sample gives better control in equating the experimental and control groups. Biases are factors which distort conclusions. Research is filled with uncertainty which is eliminated to a degree with the use of experimental design.

Sampling

What is a Population?

A population may be defined as a set of data that consists of all conceivably (or hypothetically) possible observations of a certain phenomenon.[7] A bushel of two dent-shelled corn or prices paid for compact cars are examples of populations. The components in the first population cited are homogeneous. In the second example, prices paid for compact cars vary with each manufacturer and, therefore, are heterogeneous in nature.

Censuses and surveys are commonly conducted with populations that are heterogeneous. The censuses of populations, industrial production, and agriculture are aggregates embracing large numbers of separate units that are often dissimilar in various respects.[8]

Populations are classified as finite or infinite. A finite population consists of a definite number of objects, as contrast to an infinite population which is indefinitely large.

What is a Sample?

"Sampling, that is the selection of an aggregate of material to represent the whole aggregate, is a long-established practice."[9] One of the first attempts to gather agricultural data by sampling was used by George Washington in 1771. Washington used a circular letter to gather data informing him on prices of land, livestock, poultry, and produce. This circular letter was sent to several gentleman farmers who had both the knowledge and judgement for answering the questions.

A simple example of a sample is the selection of a pint of grain from a bushel of grain. As discussed previously, grain may be considered homogeneous in nature and the sample, if not too small, will be a very close representative of the population. However, when the population to be sampled consists of units that tend to be heterogeneous in nature, then a sophisticated selection process is needed.[10]

Samples may be classified as being either random or judgement, depending on the method of selection. The random sample is the only sample that contains reliable information about a population. In the selection of random samples, it is assumed that every individual in the population has a known probability of appearing in the sample. The selection cannot be left to the discretion of the sampler, since the probability of his selection cannot be determined.[11]

The area sample and stratified random sample arc examples of modified random samples. The area sample is performed by dividing the population into scgments, and then taking a random sample of segments. The sample segments may be completely enumerated or samples may be drawn within the segments. Block sampling, a form of area sampling, refers to the process of complete enumeration of the sample segments.[12] The stratified random sample is achieved by arranging the population into groups or strata in which portions are allocated towards the total sample.[13]

A judgement sample utilizes personal judgement in the selection of the sample. For example, Toyota Co. might feel that the consumers in Nagoya are typical of consumers in Japan. This survey based solely on Nagoya would constitute a judgement sample if the generalizations for Japan are based on Nagoya. A disadvantage of judgement samples is that an evaluation of estimates and decisions must also be based on judgement.[14]

Quota sampling is essentially a judgement sample, since it depends on the choice of the interviewer to fulfil the quota. Due to biased selection, the sample estimates of the population parameters cannot be tested statistically.[15]

Why Sample of Population?

Today's public is affected in a variety of ways by sampling. Public opinion polls are reported in newspapers, quality control is maintained by manufacturers, and even the Census offices utilize a well-developed sampling programme.[16]

There are a variety of reasons why populations are sampled, as opposed to the alternative of an exhaustive enumeration. An exhaustive enumeration would be impossible in the case of an infinite population and unfeasible in many cases because of high cost. In some cases exhaustive enumerations are unnecessary and impractical. Reasonably accurate results can be obtained with less cost and time involved by the use of random samples.[17]

In the case of a small population, it may be more convenient to collect data from the whole population instead of sampling.[18] In this case, an exhaustive enumeration would provide data that corresponded to that of the measurements made on the population.

Procedure for Sampling

"The principle object of any sampling procedure is to secure a sample which, subject to limitations of size, will reproduce the characteristics of the population, especially those of immediate interest, as closely as possible."[19]

Purpose of Study

Before a sample technique can be determined, the problem and population must be clearly defined. A decision must be made concerning the information desired. Next the decision will have to be made to determine whether a survey will be of any value in providing the information needed.

Sample Design

"*A* sample design is a definite plan, completely determined before any data are collected, for obtaining a sample from a given population."[20]

In the past, farm production economists have argued whether the random or block sample provided the best estimation of the mean values or frequency distributions of a sample population. If the main objective of a survey is to estimate the mean parameter, then the random (or stratified random) sampie is the most efficient. If, however, the objective is to compare the means of two or more discrete populations, a random sample should be taken from each population.[21]

Sample Size

In the statistical sampling that is carried on by the government or corporations, there are six criteria that have to be met.

1. Usefulness and comprehensiveness of content.
2. Reliability of results, sufficient for the purpose.
3. Intelligibility (classifications and definitions understood).
4. Speed.
5. Economy of operation.
6. Accurate interpretation and presentation.

Most of the above criteria will be satisfied by establishing a good technique for determining the proper sample size.

By using a pilot survey the economist can pretest, compare, and revise different versions of the questionnaire. The pilot survey will also yield advance estimates of parameters needed to determine the appropriate sample size, so that the cost of the survey will be a minimum.

For example, if an economist decided to compare methods of mechanical harvesting of corn for grain, he would use a pilot survey to determine the variance of harvesting with a corn-picker, plus the variance of harvesting with a picker-sheller. (Possibly a review of literature could provide this information.) After the variances have been determined, a simple statistical formula, can be used to determine estimates of desired parameters and finally the appropriate sample size. In the preceding example it would not be inappropriate to use samples of equal size since the study is a comparison of two methods of harvesting.[22]

The simplest way of avoiding bias in selecting the sample is to draw the sample at random. By placing certain restrictions[23] on a random sample, the accuracy will improve if bias is not introduced into the results.[24]

In estimating regression relationships of a population the stratified random sample is the most appropriate. The regression coefficients are similar to means since they are population parameters. The stratified random sample restricts the sample selection to an equal number of cases that are drawn at random within each interval for an entire population.[25]

Observation and Description of Data

Direct information is collected by personal interviews, telephone calls, mail questionnaires, or some combination of the three. In general, the mail questionnaire is more economical and convenient for contacting homes and firms that are widely dispersed. Personal interviews have the advantage of obtaining information that is hard to get by mail questionnaire (i.e., income data) specially in countries where large number of people are illiterate.

In statistical studies the characteristics observed may be either measurable or non-measurable. Some fundamental characteristics that are measurable are length, weight, and time. In measuring, the *extent* or *amount* of a characteristic associated with a given element are observed. The recorded observations and computations relating to measured characteristics are commonly called measurement data.

In the case of non-measurable data, it is impossible to determine amounts associated with each element in the sample or population. However, these data can be handled by using numbers to count the elements possessing a given characteristic. These data are termed attribute data.

Drawing the Inference and Stating the Precision

When generalizations for populations are concluded from samples, the inference is determined through a process of inductive reasoning. Inductive reasoning implies reasoning from the particular to the general.[26]

There are fundamentally two way of stating the inference from a random sample: (1) the point estimate; and (2) the interval estimate. In using the point estimate, it is assumed that the sample infers the same facts that are contained in the population. In the interval estimate, the probability that a fact lies within the confidence interval is indicated in terms of per cent.[27]

Statisticians use a variety of tests to state the precision of various experiments. Examples of tests that are commonly performed are chi square[28] student's "t" test, the normal curve approximation, and the "f" tests.[29]

The Summing Up

Before a sample technique can be determined, the population and its associated problem must first be clearly defined. Information needed to arrive at a satisfactory solution to the problem must then be determined. Next, a sampling procedure must be formulated to provide the necessary information at the lowest possible cost. The sample size and design will greatly influence the sample, since the sample for a good statistical programme is based on the criteria listed below.[30]

1. Usefulness and comprehensiveness of content.
2. Reliability of results, sufficient for the purpose.
3. Intelligibility (classifications and definitions understood).
4. Speed.
5. Economy of operation.
6. Accurate interpretation and presentation.

Sample selection is very important, since a biased sample will lead to invalid generalizations. A random sample or a modified random sample is the only certain way of avoiding bias in sampling. In using a modified random sample, the research worker must be careful that he does not introduce bias in the results.

Direct information may be collected and presented in a variety of ways, depending on the population and information desired. After the data are collected and tabulated, the inference may be drawn and presented as a point estimate or an interval estimate.

Interview Techniques

The interview is a most widely used method of gathering information in the field. No other approach enables the investigator to glean so much information and yet remains so flexible.

The problem solving sequence adopted in research involves: (1) formulating the problem, (2) determining source material, (3) preparing data collection forms, (4) designing the sample, (5) collecting the data in the field, and (6) editing, coding, tabulating and analysing the results. Clearly interview procedures to be used at each level remain much the same; but objectives may differ greatly. Hence, a clear distinction between each type of study becomes necessary, not in discussing technique as such, but to have a well-conceived plan of study to be properly executed.

Exploratory research or reconnaissance is concerned with formulating and crystallizing the problem for further study. It is a means of gathering initial information. The interview itself is the most important method of gathering such background information in the field.

Descriptive study needs the collection of information in the field according to formal design. Interviews at this level are conducted according to formal plan in an attempt to reach the highest levels of accuracy and validity. The interviewer often works within a specific sample design with a prepared questionnaire. Each interview is conducted in a similar manner in order to retain a measure of comparison between each response. The information sought must be conducted accordingly.

Field work in exploratory research is almost exclusively the realm of the interviewer. The object of exploratory interviewing is to find new ideas and hence many of the restrictions common to formal interviewing may and should be eliminated. Conduct of the interview is totally at the interviewer's discretion. Exploratory interviewing is nothing more than an informal survey of all individuals who are apt to have new or differing ideas on the subject under study. By contacting many informed sources the necessary information prerequisite to the formal execution of the study is compiled. The enlightened person, usually of position or authority, is often of greatest value.

Several rules apply exclusively to this form of interview. Most importantly one should not limit interviews to persons of one given class. Members of the same social or economic background would tend to give similar responses to questions asked. The basic idea of this form of interview is not to seek similarity of answers, but rather to seek a great diversity of response. Reactions need not be representative nor express a common view rather each idea expressed is valued for its own content. It is best that all published and other secondary sources be surveyed prior to the interview. A minimum knowledge of the subject should be acquired and questions asked to the interviewee should be properly developed. Finally, once a particular interview nears completion the interviewer should ask for further references. The researcher should follow each lead until either a dead end is reached or the necessary information is compiled.

Less latitude is permitted in conducting an interview when proceeding with a formally designed study. The most carefully chosen method of sampling and well thought schedules are worthless if an interview is poorly conducted. The techniques used to obtain true answers should be given careful thought and the method of interviewing chosen wisely.

There are several ways of conducting an interview. The most common are as follows:

1. *The Free Story:* The interviewer is encouraged to tell his story in narrative form. Few questions are asked. This results in a mass of notes, biased toward the interviewer, which are seldom usable in quantitative form.
2. *Aided Recall, Recognition and Identification:* This is used primarily in advertising surveys. The respondent is shown a list or series of pictures and pertinent questions are then asked.
3. *Focused Interview:* The interviewer carries a schedule in hand and has a few leading questions ready to encourage the respondent. The answers should be recorded

verbatim. The results are usually biased toward the interviewer, but provide a wealth of illustrative material.

In development research the focused interview is generally used. However, a good method of interviewing is useless if the interviewer does not know what he is doing. There are many things to understand. The final results must be reliable, relevant and representative. An interview is a dynamic process, "conversation directed to a definite purpose". There must be active participation on the part of both the interviewer and the interviewee, but more is expected of the interviewer. He is the one guiding the conversation.

He must be aware of the ever present bias toward his likes and dislikes which is often matched by inaccuracies due to unwillingness, prejudice, ignorance or inarticulatedness on the part of the respondent.

Communication is a basic problem. People speak with gestures, expressions, tones of voice and silences. The interviewer must be able to evaluate these as they provide the shades of meaning that lie behind the plain words. There are also obstructions to communication as well as aids. These are used without conscious knowledge most of the time. In the years spent learning to communicate, people have also learnt ways to hinder it. These ways are designed to avoid revealing undesirable facts or to avoid unwanted influence.

Anticipation is another such hindrance. People try to guess what the next words of the speaker will be and as a result fail to listen to what is actually said and then give inaccurate answers. It is impossible for people to accept a question at face value. Long communication has taught that words seldom say everything and so much energy is expended evaluating the question in terms of what it or the answer means to the respondent before the answer can be verbalized.

These blocks to communication are present on the part of both the interviewer and the respondent. Those of the interviewer result in creating forces' that lead toward inaccuracies and distorted communication. For example, approval in the form of a smile or a nod of the head suggests to the respondent that this was a good answer and should be repeated or overemphasized. Disapproval indicates to the respondent that he should avoid such kinds of answers in the future.

There are other barriers to a good interview. Memory loss is a common one. The greater the period of time between the event and the question the more the person has forgotten or changed his memory of the event.

There are many other barriers, but there are aids as well. Most people are not only willing, but anxious to be helpful and if the interviewer can establish good rapport in the beginning of the interview most of these barriers will disappear or at least diminish.

Professional interviewers have set up long lists of do's and don'ts to help the non-professional break down these barriers and succeed with the interview:

1. Learn as much as possible about the interviewee.
2. Make an appointment.
3. Provide for reasonable privacy.
4. Establish a relationship of confidence that is not one-sided.
5. Listen. Do not air your own opinions.
6. Maintain control of the conversation. Do not go off at a tangent.
7. Be straightforward and frank.
8. Allow enough time, but do not dawdle.

9. One question at a time and get the full answer.
10. Record all data as soon as possible.
11. Get all the facts and then close the interview gracefully.
12. Use simple nuclear words.

Following these rules will help, but not guarantee a good interview. Every interviewer will have good and bad interviews; sometimes all the rules can be broken and results will still be good. There is no given formula to be used universally. Every beginner feels as though no other person has ever faced the situation before. The primary rule of establishing good rapport and then using one's common sense well usually makes the differences between success and failure.

Notes

1. Jahoda, Marie, Deutsch, Morton and Cook, Stuart W., *Research Methods in Social Relations,* New York: Dryden, 1951, p. 63.
2. *Ibid.*
3. *Op. cit.*
4. E.B. Wilson, *Introduction to Scientific Research,* New York: McGraw-Hill, 1952, Chapter 3.
5. Jahoda, Deutsch, and Cook, *op. cit.*
6. *Ibid.*
7. John E. Freund and Frank J. Williams, *Modern Business Statistics,* Englewood Cliffs, N.J.: Prentice-Hall, p. 43.
8. Frank Yates, *Sampling Methods for Censuses and Surveys,* 3rd rev. ed., New York: Habner, 1965 p. 2.
9. Yates, *op. cit.,* p. 1.
10. *Ibid.*
11. George W. Snedecor, and W.G. Cochran, *Statistical Methods,* 7th ed., Amer: Jowa State Univ. Press, 1980, p. 7.

12. Earl O. Heady, "Methods in Farm Production Economics Research", *Journal of Farm Economics,* 30 May 1948, p. 223.
13. Freund and Williams, *op. cit.,* p. 279.
14. *Ibid.,* p. 240.
15. *Ibid.,* p. 281.
16. Snedecor, *op. cit.,* p. 1.
17. Freund and Williams, *op. cit.,* p. 172.
18. William G. Cochran, "Design and Analysis of Sampling", in Snedecor and Cochran, *Statistical Methods,* p.490.
19. Yates, *op. cit.,* p. 9.
20. Freund and Williams, *op. cit.,* p. 279.
21. Heady, *op. cit.,* p. 222.
22. *Ibid.*
23. An excellent example of a modified random sample is the serpentine pattern used in John L. Crothers and Creighton N. Guellow, *Laying Flocks in Maryland,* College Park: University of Maryland, 1958. Misc. Ext. Pub. No. 43.
24. Yates, *op. cit.,* p. 10.
25. Heady, *op. cit.,* p. 223.
26. Snedecor, *op. cit.,* p. 2.
27. *Ibid.*
28. Freund and Williams provide an excellent discussion of Chi square, *op. cit.,* p. 248.
29. Freund and Williams provide a discussion of the "*f*" test, *op. cit.,* Chapter II.
30. Deming, *op. cit.,* p. 3.

5

Preparing a Research Project

Formulating the Project Idea

Researchers interested in taking up research have the initial difficulty of picking up a problem worth investigating. At times they waste considerable amount of time in just thinking about the pros and cons of problems suggested by different persons. This indecision usually results from certain misunderstandings about "What is research"? Usual notion about research is that it must result in something spectacular; it must come up with a new discovery or theory.

It must be pointed out here that a study which brings forward new facts, or generalizations or which demolishes or establishes a hypothesis or a theory or a principle already in vogue, or which puts a variety of information into an order or system, or which prepares grounds for further research is as valid a research as one which ends with a new discovery or theory.

As mentioned earlier, research can be of two types: (1) fundamental, and (2) applied. The latter is done to understand the processes through which a certain constructive programme can be successfully applied, whereas, the former is solely devoted to the understanding of the basic principles underlying a phenomenon and is not directly concerned with its application and usefulness. In actual practice the two are, however, not always separable. Whether a researcher should engage himself in fundamental or applied research, will depend solely upon his research interest, orientation, and training together with the purpose of his research.

The best problem for research is one which arises from the researcher's own curiosity. He can handle a topic in which he is really interested better than the one suggested by someone else. This has, however, to be qualified by an equally important element. The researcher must know the tools which can handle the problems he proposes to take up.

Before choosing the problem for research one should, therefore, ask the following questions to himself:

1. Is this problem really of interest to me?
2. Is it significant in the sense that it extends the frontiers of knowledge or fills an important gap in knowledge?
3. Can I handle this problem within the constraints of resources of (money, time and others) available?
4. Has this problem not been investigated by someone else?

After the problem has been identified, it should be put in the form of a proposal which should cover the following:

A. Describe problem situation or problem areas:
    1. Indicate conditions which give rise to the problem.
    2. Indicate individuals or groups which are affected.
    3. Indicate specifically how each individual or group is affected.
    4. Briefly, describe previous work in this area. Point out the extent to which satisfactory solutions exist, shortcomings in methodology, etc.

B. State the problem to be investigated in clear and concise terms. These may be called specific objectives of this project:

C. Present justification of these objectives by:

   1. Relating specific objectives to problem area.
   2. Indicating the manner in which "users" could apply answers in making decisions.

D. Collection of data:

   1. Indicate the kinds and amount of data needed to solve the problem, accomplish the objectives, or test the hypotheses.
   2. Indicate where and how the data will be obtained. If data are to be obtained from survey, develop a questionnaire.

E. Analysis:

   1. Describe the manner in which data will be analysed:
      (a) Indicate what relationships will be tested.
      (b) Indicate criteria for establishment of relationships. (For example, what conditions must exist to support the conclusion that variable *A* is or is not related to variable *B*.)

General Comments

Research projects vary so widely in nature and scope that it is difficult to develop a specific outline to serve all purposes. Therefore, this general outline should be modified and adapted for the particular project. The above outline could be stated as follows:

A. Development of theoretical framework.

B. Statement of hypotheses which are based on I-A.

C. Justification.

D. Collection of data.

E. Analysis of data and test of hypotheses.

Defining the Problem

In order to maximise their research results, students must be clear about the purpose, the objectives and the scope of their research projects and must be sure of the research methods they can possibly use. It is, therefore, important that these initial steps be planned and thought out carefully before a research project is taken up for study.

There are various purposes for which research is done. Generally speaking, a post-graduate student has to conduct research in order to fulfil an assignment given by his professor or to meet the requirements of a post-graduate degree. At times research is conducted to satisfy one's own curiosity and interest, while at other times it is done as a commercial venture. No matter what the purpose, the end product of all researches is either a new insight into the problem under investigation or a new method of approaching the problem or a new order or system of data hitherto available only in a haphazard way. The prior and clear understanding of the purpose for which research is proposed to be done, enables the researcher to formulate his objective and research design more specifically and appropriately.

The success of a researcher is largely determined by his ability to meet the objectives of his research project. It is, therefore, important that the objective or objectives of a research project be stated unambiguously and at the very outset. While stating the objectives, the researcher is expected to state "what he wants to find out" and what does he mean by "what he wants to find out". More often than not, it is not difficult to define one's objectives in a theoretical sense but it is difficult to define them operationally. Let us take the example of a student who wants to find out the impact of culture on the land use pattern of an area. He may state his objective in the following term: *"To find out the impact of culture on the land use pattern of X area".* It seems as if the objective has been very clearly stated. But it is not so. It is really very ambiguous. The student has not yet given the theoretical and operational definition of the terms "culture" and "land use". Culture may mean different things to different people. After giving the theoretical meaning of the term "culture", he will have to state how he is going to measure it in order to determine its impact on the land use pattern of the area in question. In other words he will have to back his theoretical definition of the term 'culture' by its operational definition. He will have to do the same thing with regard to other terms.

In addition to the clear understanding and statement of the purpose and objectives of research, students should also know the scope of their research and the methods which can be used to meet the objectives of the project. All these preliminaries should be so stated that the reader is not left in doubt about the intentions of the researcher.

Preparing a Tentative Outline

The next step in the process of research is to prepare a tentative outline, which can be used as a framework for collecting research data. A well thought out outline should clearly reflect the purpose, objective and scope of research and the order in which the contents of the report are to be presented.

An outline may be divided into parts, chapters and sub-headings. The structure of the outline will be determined by the nature of research output one is aiming at. A long report will consist of several chapters. But a research paper to be published in a professional journal will have only sub-headings. Ordinarily, the first chapter should be an introduction which contains statements of purpose, objectives, scope and methods of research and the organization of the report. The order in which the chapters and sub-headings are placed in the outline should be logical and rational so that the flow of thought is orderly. The sub-headings should not deviate from the main objective of the chapters under which they appear (Fig. 5.1).

CHAPTER I — INTRODUCTION

- Purpose, Objective and Scope
- Methods of Research
- Organization

CHAPTER II. — THE LAND AND THE PEOPLE

- The Land
    - Land forms
    - Climate
        - Temperature
        - Rainfall
        - Others
- Soils

Fig. 5.1: The Order of Chapters and Sub-headings

After the preparation of the outline, one should look for sources of information relevant to the research project.

Data Sources and Data Collection

After the project idea has been settled, one should begin a serious search for the sources of information. Usually there are two main sources of information.

1. Field investigation; and
2. Library research.

Which of the two sources should be tapped by a researcher, will depend upon the nature of his research project. If it involves field work, he will have to chalk out a programme and methods of investigation. If it is based on library research and desk work, he will have to concentrate on secondary sources of information. Most projects involve both field investigation and library research. Researchers should, therefore, know the methods of handling both.

The first step in any research is the picking of the general sources of information for basic understanding of the problem.

The Literature Search

One can get a number of relevant and useful references in the encyclopaedia, index to periodicals, and a few professional periodicals. A suggested list of such sources is given below:

1. Encyclopaedia Britannica,
2. Encyclopaedia of Social Sciences,
3. International and national indices to periodicals,
4. Bibliographies,
5. National and international journals, and
6. Library catalogue.

Most of these sources are available in almost all university libraries including the one of the University of Mysore.

The nature of the research project will, of course, influence the kind of literature the researcher will look for. If his project concerns an aspect of physical planning, he would choose a different set of sources than would be the case if he were considering an aspect of economics. If the project concerns a small area, an encyclopaedia may not be of much help and he may have to depend on official reports, occasional publications and, of course, on his own field investigations.

How to Look into Encyclopaedia and Indices?

Selecting Key Words

In order to save time, it is better to write down a set of key words on a 5″ × 8″ card. If a paper is entitled "Land Use in South-East Asia—Problems and Prospects", the key word card may at first, look like Fig. 2.

Key Words:
Asia
South-East Asia
Land Tenure
Land Utilization
China
Japan
Indo-China
Cambodia

Fig. 5.2: Sample of a Key Word Card

One may add other terms like Thailand, rice, soils, tropics, monsoon and so on. While looking into one of the references found under a key word, one can easily pick up other terms which can be potentially useful.

The researcher should look for these key words in the encyclopaedia of index he examines. He should add to and eliminate words from the list of key words as his knowledge of the sophistication on the topic increases. He should note down the references given at the tail end of the articles and also read the articles wherever they appear to be relevant to the topic.

Preparing a Check List

One cannot make a systematic search for literature unless one keeps a complete and accurate record of the sources consulted. It is, therefore, essential to keep a running account of such sources. How to do it, is shown in Fig. 5.3. The check list should give the date on which a particular source was consulted, and the pages consulted. It should also indicate whether references were listed there.

Check List

Britannica	1958 AD. Feb. 10.	
	Japan	Industry, population, government, administration agriculture, defence (no bibliography)
	Indo-China	Feb. 11.
		Land use, (bibliography)

Fig. 5.3: The Check List

It is definitely desirable to check out the most recently published materials first because such materials will send to additional materials published earlier.

Preparing a Bibliography Card

Each time one comes across a reference-book, articles, report, etc., useful to the research project, one should copy down all the information needed for the bibliographic reference in the final draft of the research report. Each bibliographic item should be put on a separate 5″ × 8″ card in the form as shown in Fig. 5.4.

Graham, Edward H.	Library Accession No. ....
Natural Principles of Land Use	
London: Oxford University Press, 1944	
The book is written upon the premise that biological concepts can contribute importantly to the wise use and management of land	

Fig. 5.4: A Bibliography Card

At times it is possible to have a look at the reference. In such a case it is better to put a short abstract on the bibliography card to remind oneself what to expect of the source when one looks it up later. If it is not available readily, the abstract can be prepared at the time of preparing notes from the reference. Enough space should be left in the right hand corner of the bibliography card to write the library accession number. For his own convenience researcher should set up some sort of style of his own, putting each different item of information at a different place in the card. He should perfect his style the first time he writes down the reference for bibliography. This will save a lot of time later on.

In case a researcher is planning to do a sample study requiring interviews with a number of persons, he can write the name of persons, their addresses and their relevant characteristics in the card. For efficiency sake it will be better to keep these address cards separate from the bibliography cards.

The bibliography cards should be filed alphabetically under relevant alphabetic index cards, a set of which every researcher is supposed to have and a form of which is given in Fig. 5.5.

S	T	U	V	W	XYZ
M	N	O	P	Q	R
G	H	I	J	K	L
A	B	C	D	E	F

Fig. 5.5: Sample of an Alphabetic Index Card

Preparing Notes

Systematising the Procedure

Before starting the preparation of notes, the researcher should transfer the essence of his outline to the index tabs and attach these tabs to 5″ × 8″ cards (Fig. 5.6). It is also possible to buy ready made index cards without alphabets.

A researcher has the choice of using either the 5″ × 8″ cards with index tabs affixed on the ready made index cards available in the market. In any case, he should write down the outline of his report on the tabs of the cards as shown in Fig. 5.6 and arrange these cards in the same order as the outline. This will form his outline file.

Using the Scratch Pad

After these cards are put in order, he is ready to prepare notes from the references he has noted on the bibliography cards. As he checks his actual bibliographic sources, he should keep one of his 5″ × 8″ scratch pads in hand. On the left of the top sheet of the pad he should write down the name of the author and the year of publication. As he peruses the sources he should make his notes on these sheets. He should identify the location of each note by writing the page number(s) next to the note (Fig. 5.7).

Chapter 1	*Chapter 2*	*Chapter 3*	*Chapter 4*	*Chapter 5*	*Chapter 6*

Fig. 5.6: Sample of an Index Card

Boeke, 1953

3 Boeke defined a dual economy as one where "Simultaneously two or more social systems appear...and each dominate a part of the society".

Fig. 5.7: Sample of a Page from the Scratch Pad

The researcher should make a point to put only one idea on a sheet of the scratch pad. And each time an idea is put, it should be identified by noting the last name of the writer and the page number of the book (Fig. 5.7). After the notes are completed, they should be filed under appropriate section in the outline file. And as soon as a source has been consulted, a mark should be made on the relevant bibliography card as a reminder that particular reference has already been consulted.

If during the process of preparing notes, a researcher comes across additional references for his key words card and additional ideas for his outline, he should continue to include them at appropriate places. He should not, however, forget his original objective in this process by looking for ideas not so useful for his project, although very interesting and valuable otherwise.

While going through the preparation of notes and the field work, the researcher may get some ideas from his associates, professors, colleagues or friends. He himself may think of something while sitting alone and meditating. He should immediately note down these ideas on the scratch pad and file them at the appropriate place in the outline file.

If there is considerable amount of facts and figures that need to be analysed, the researcher should complete the analysis and file the results in the outline file. If there are certain maps or diagrams to be included in the paper they should be noted on the scratch pad and filed.

Field Work

Field work provides the primary data for research. Researchers without adequate background, often neglect the preparatory work necessary before any field work can be conducted. One must decide precisely the nature and type of data needed, the procedure of gathering the data, the format of the data and the analytical tools to be utilized for the data analysis.

There are two basic procedures for data gathering: (1) census, and (2) sample. In the case of census, information is gathered from all the units of the "population" or "universe". Whereas, in the case of sample, only selected units are observed. It is rarely that a researcher uses census method unless his object/ problem of research is too localized and micro and he can handle all the units without difficulty. This may be the case when the study of a single village is done.

More about these has been discussed earlier.

6

Statistical Analysis of Data

The individual sets of data whether collected from secondary sources or field surveys are discrete; they have to be summarized and then analyzed to get patterns and trends. The first step in summarization and analysis is the determination of central tendencies: they are:

1. Arithmetic mean or average,
2. Median,
3. Mode, and
4. Geometric mean.

Arithmetic Mean

Arithmetic Mean is the most commonly used to calculate central tendency that generalizes a series of data of the same type. Here is a simple example. Suppose we have the following set of data giving the number of years ten persons of a village lived in cities: 1, 4, 4, 3, 10, 3, 5, 20, 4, and 6. If we add these discrete numbers, and divide the total by the number of people involved, we get (60/10) = 6. This is the arithmetic mean or average of the number of years the persons surveyed who lived in cities.

Arithmetic Mean can be expressed as:

$$\bar{X} = \frac{\Sigma X}{N}$$

where $\bar{X}$ = arithmetic mean

X = individual values making up the series of data

N = frequencies (number of items)

Σ = (Sigma) the summation or total of all the values of X

This formula is applicable only if the data are given in discrete forms. In case of grouped data, a different formula is used. Given below are the formula and its application.

Table 6.1 gives the sales checks of a Grocery Store in a grouped format. We have to calculate the arithmetic mean.

Table 6.1: Sales Checks in a Grocery Store

Class	*Mid-point*	*Class frequency*	*Frequency × Mid-point*
	X	*f*	*fX*
₹ 1 and < 3	2	3	₹ 6
₹ 3 and < 5	4	9	₹ 36
₹ 5 and < 7	6	25	₹ 150
₹ 7 and < 9	8	35	₹ 280
₹ 9 and < 11	10	17	₹ 170
₹ 11 and < 13	12	10	₹ 120
₹ 13 and < 15	14	1	₹ 14
		100	₹ 776

Formula for the grouped data is as follows:

$$\bar{X} = \frac{\Sigma fX}{N}$$

$$N = 100 \; \Sigma fX = ₹\, 776$$

Substituting the numbers, we get

$$\bar{X} = \frac{\Sigma fX}{N} N = \frac{₹\,776}{100} = ₹\,7.76$$

Thus, the mean sale value for the store is ₹ 7.76.

Median

Median represents the mean expectation in that there are as many individual occurrences above it as there are below it. In the calculation of the median every occurrence is given the same weight, i.e., it is regarded as of equal importance no matter of what magnitude it is. This means that widely differing sets of data can return the same median value. Further this implies that the median possesses no real mathematical qualities and cannot be used for further computations.

If we arrange the data showing the number of years, another set of ten persons lived in cities in the following order: 1, 2, 2, 3, **3**, 3, 4, 5, and 5 and try to find the mid-value by observation, we get 3 as there are four figures to the left and the same number to the right of 3. The mid-value of a given set of data is called Median. In this case it is 3. The Arithmetic Mean of the same set of data would be 28/9 = 3.11. If we take into account the frequency of the figures in the series and select the one, which occurs most often, we get 3. The figure with highest number of occurrences in a series is called Mode. In this particular case 3 occurs three times. While arithmetic mean represents the series best, the median and mode too represent the series to some extent at least.

We will now go into details:

Value	*Frequency*
1	1
2	2
3	3
4	1
5	2

To reiterate, median is that value of a variable which lies midway when the data are arranged in order of magnitude. Median value of n observations will be $(n + 1)1/2$ of the observation. *Example*: To find the Median of (12, 3 and 6), first we put them in order of magnitude (3, 6, 12). The middle number is 6, so the median is 6. Here is another example: Given below are 15 numbers: 3, 13, 7, 5, 21, 23, 39, 23, 40, 23, 14, 12, 56, 23, and 29. If we put them in order, we get: 3, 5, 7, 12, 13, 14, 21, 23, 23, 23, 23, 29, 39, 40, and 56. In this set of 15 numbers, the medium number is 23. We see that "half the numbers in the list are less, and half the numbers are greater than 23". It matters little if some numbers are listed more than once in the list.

If the total observations amount to even numbers, the calculation of the median will be slightly different. In that case, we would try to find the middle pair of numbers, and then add them and divide by two. Here is an example. Fourteen discrete numbers: 3, 13, 7, 5, 21, 23, 23, 40, 23, 14, 12, 56, 23, and 29 are then put in ascending order: 3, 5, 7, 12, 13, 14, 21, 23, 23, 23, 23, 29, 40, and 56. In this case, we do not have a middle number but we do have a pair of middle numbers: 21 and 23. We add them and divide by two to get the median value, i.e., 21 + 23 = 44 ÷ 2 = 22. And, so, the Median, in this case is **22**. It is a number, which is not in the list but it does meet one criterion: half the numbers in the list are less, and the other half more than 22.

In the case of grouped data, the following formula is used:

$$\text{Median} = L_1 + \left(\frac{\frac{N}{2} - \Sigma f_1}{fm} \right) \cdot X$$

where L_1 = lower limit of the median class.

N = total frequency

Σf_1 = the sum of all frequencies accumulated before entering the median class.

fm = the frequencies in the median class.

X = the size of the class interval of the median class.

Method of finding the median of grouped data using the above formula is exemplified by Table 6.2, which gives the number of workers in various industrial establishments.

Table 6.2: Number of Industrial Establishments and Number of Workers

Number of Workers	*No. of Establishments (= frequencies)*	*Cumulative Frequency*
0 - 49	46	46
50 - 99	59	105
100 - 149	45	150
150 - 199	37	187
200 - 299	31	218
300 - 399	20	238
400 - 499	13	251
500 and over	9	260

$$N = 260$$

$$\frac{N}{2} = 130$$

$$L_1 = 100$$

$$\Sigma f_1 = 105$$

$$fm = 45$$

$$X = 50$$

$$\text{Median} = 100 + \left(\frac{130 - 105}{45}\right) \cdot 50$$

$$= 127.78 \text{ workers}$$

As apparent from the above example, a median divides the data into two equal parts. It is called 02 i.e. second quartile. Quartiles that mark the limits of lower and upper quarters are known as 1st and 3rd quartiles respectively. Similarly, particular values, which divide the total observations into 10 and 100 equal parts, are respectively known as deciles and percentiles. The quartiles are denoted by Q_1, Q_2... Q_n whereas deciles and percentiles by D_1, D_2... D_n and P_1, P_2... P_n, etc.

The quartile observations are ascertained by the formula:

$$Q_1 = \frac{n+1}{4} \text{ th observation}$$

$$Q_2 = \frac{n+1}{2} \text{ th observation}$$

$$Q_3 = \frac{3(n+1)}{4} \text{ th observation}$$

If the series is a discrete one, the values can be computed using the following formula:

$$Q = L_1 + \left(\frac{L_2 + L_1}{F}\right)(q - c)$$

where L_2 and L_1 are upper and lower limits of the quartile class

F = frequency of the quartile class.

q = quartile observation.

c = cumulative frequency preceding the quartile class.

Similarly, there are methods to calculate deciles and percentiles.

$$D_1 = \frac{n+1}{10} \text{ th observation}$$

$$D_9 = 9\frac{(n+1)}{10} \text{ th observation}$$

$$D = L_1 + \frac{L_2 + L_1}{F}(d - c)$$

$$P_1 = \frac{(n+1)}{100} \text{th observation}$$

$$P_{50} = 50\frac{(n+1)}{100} \text{th observation}$$

$$P = L_1 + \frac{L_2 + L_1}{F}(p - c)$$

The above derivations prove that Median = $Q_2 = D_5 = P_{50}$

Mode

Mode is a value, which occurs most often in a given distribution. In a grouped data, the class having the maximum frequency is called modal class. The mode, by its very definition indicates what is most common or frequent. Very often, however, there are difficulties in deciding exactly where the mode is. This may be either because the data are multi-modal or the choice of the class is biased.

Comparing Mean, Median and Mode

Among the three types of averages, arithmetic mean alone is suitable for mathematical analysis. The first step in calculating the mean is to assign weight to each occurrence according to its magnitude and then add them together and divide them by the number of occurrences. For example, if the output of one farm is 200 quintals and that of another farm is 100 quintals, the average output of each farm would be 150 quintals. This, however, does not give a real picture. For a proper appreciation of the reality underlying a mean value, it is necessary to know how the individual variates summarize the mean.

The formula for the grouped data is:

$$\text{Mode} = L_1 + \frac{\Delta_1}{\Delta_1 + \Delta_2} \cdot X$$

where L_1 = the lower limit of the modal class.

Δ_1 = differences between the frequencies in the modal class and pre-modal class.

Δ_2 = the difference between the frequencies in the modal class and post-modal class.

X = the size of the class interval of the modal class.

To find the mode we may take the example given in Table 6.3.

Table 6.3: Finding the Mode of Weekly Income of Workers

Weekly income (₹)	*No. of Workers*
10 and < 20	85
20 and < 30	120
30 and < 40	110
40 and < 50	67
50 and < 60	49
60 and < 70	21
70 and < 80	6
All	**458**

Here $L_1 = 20$; $\Delta_1 = 35$; $\Delta_2 = 10$; $X = 10$

(*Note*: the modal class is the class with largest frequencies; in this case it is 120.

$$\text{Mode} = 20 + \left(\frac{35}{35+10}\right)10$$

$$= 20 + 7.78 = ₹\ 27.78$$

Geometric Mean

The geometric mean is the nth root of the product of N items. It helps in averaging the ratios and in computing average rates of increase or decrease. To compute the geometric mean to two items, we take the square root; if three items, the cube root, and so on. Geometric mean can be used only if the series being analyzed does not contain zeros or negative values.

The formula for geometric mean is $G = n^{th}$ product of the Xs. To calculate the geometric mean of a set of data, we use the following formula:

$$\left(\prod_{i=1}^{n} a_i\right)^{1/n} = \sqrt[n]{a_1 a_2 \ldots a_n}$$

$\{a_1, a_2, \ldots, a_n\}$ is:

Thus, the geometric mean of two numbers, say 2 and 8, will be square root of their product; that is $\sqrt[2]{2 \times 8} = 4$; and the geometric mean of three numbers 1, ½, ¼ will be the cube root of their product (1/8), which is 1/2; that is,

$$\sqrt[3]{1 \times \tfrac{1}{2} \times \tfrac{1}{4}} = \tfrac{1}{2}$$

Relationship among the Central Tendencies

The average, the median and the mode are the main techniques of expressing the mean values of a set of data. The relationship among them and when and where to use them, let us consider the series 1, 2, 2, 3, 3, 3, 4, 4, 5 wherein the mean, median and mode coincide. Fig. 6.1(a) shows a histogram based on this series. The distribution shown by this histogram is called normal distribution, and the curve representing this distribution is called a normal distribution curve (Fig. 6.1(b)]. The existence of normal distribution is assumed in most statistical analysis, although in practice it seldom exists. If this series is changed to 1, 1, 2, 2, 2, 3, 3, 4, 4, and 5

$$\text{We get the Mean } \bar{X} = \Sigma X$$
$$= 27/10 = 2.7$$
$$\text{Median} = 2.5$$
$$\text{Mode} = 2$$

The distribution we get is not normal. It is skewed. If the tail extends to the right, it is called positive skewness; and if it extends to the left, it is called negative skewness (Fig. 6.1).

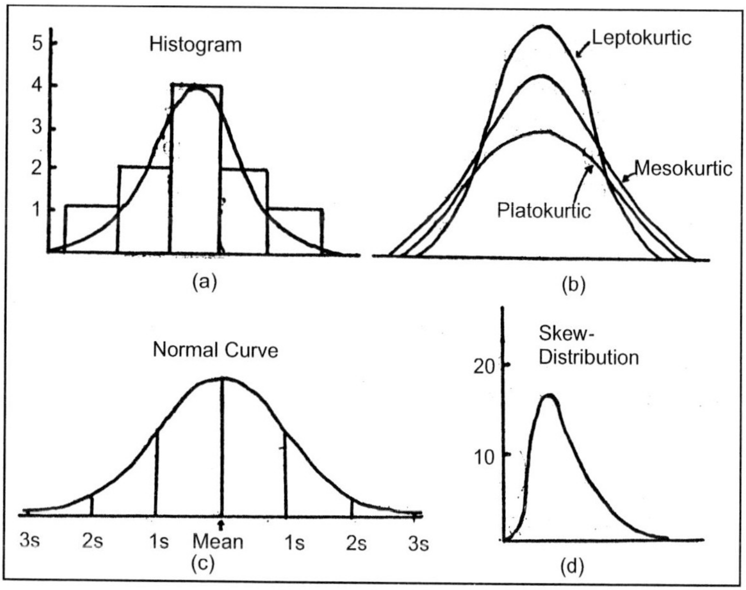

Fig. 6.1: Histogram and Various Types of Curves

Calculating Deviation from the Mean

Deviation or variability means the distances at which the variates stand from the mean. In our case, the distance at which ₹ 2000 and ₹ 1000 stand from ₹ 1500 is deviation. This can be done either by finding absolute variations i.e. ₹ 2000 – 1500 = ₹ 500, and ₹ 1000 – ₹ 1500 = – ₹ 500; or by relative differences, i.e., + 33.33 per cent and – 33.33 per cent. Absolute deviation is expressed in positional terms also.

Deviation is of two types:

1. Range, and
2. Inter-quartile.

Range Deviation: If we indicate the lowest and the highest values along with the mean value, then we give the range of deviation. For example, the following two sets of data have the same averages but different ranges.

Set A. 1, 3, 5, 7, 9: average = 5

Set B. 3, 4, 5, 6, 7: average = 5

In the first case, the range is: 1 to 9 while in the second it is: 3 to 7. If both average and range are given, it is easier to understand a series.

Inter-quartile Deviation: This is another form of scatter, which is used in conjunction with the median.

$$\text{I.Q. D.} = \frac{Q_1 - Q_2}{2}$$

Where, Q_1 and Q_2 are the upper and lower quartiles respectively.

Mean and Standard Deviation

Mean deviation and the standard deviation are the two most commonly used methods to find out absolute deviation. Both taken into account the deviation of each item in a series form an average. The average deviation tells how much each occurrence differs from the average. To find out average deviation (D), differences are added and the sum divided by the number of items (Table 6.4).

Table 6.4: Method of Calculating Average Deviation

Items	*Values* *X*	*Deviation* *D*
1	1	– 4
2	3	– 2
3	5	0
4	7	+ 2
5	9	+ 4
Total 5	25	12

$$\bar{X} \text{ (Mean)} = 1+3+5+7+9+25 = 50/5 = 5$$

$$\Sigma D \text{ (Deviation)} = -4 + -2 + 0 + 2 + 4$$

(signs ignored)

$$= 12$$

$$\text{Average (mean) deviation} = \Sigma\frac{D}{X} = \frac{12}{5} = 2.4$$

In this case, 2.4 is the mean deviation. It may be noted that in this calculation, no consideration has been given to positive and negative deviations.

Standard Deviation

As mentioned earlier, we do not take into account positive (+) and negative (–) signs while calculating the mean deviation. One way of getting over this mathematically irrational approach is to square the deviations (Table 6.5). This is what we do when we calculate the standard deviation.

Table 6.5: Number of Persons Employed and Volume of Sales in a Store

X	*D*	D^2
1	− 4	16
3	− 2	4
5	0	0
7	+ 2	4
9	+ 4	16
25/5 = 5	12	40/5 = 8

$$X = 25/5 = 5 \quad D = 12$$

Now $\Sigma D^2 = 40$

the variance $= \frac{\Sigma D^2}{N} = \frac{40}{5} = 8$

The value derived from dividing the squared deviations by the number of values is called Variance. Here 8 is the variance. If we calculate the square root of the Variance, we get a value, called Standard Deviation.

The shorthand formula for the two is given below:

$$\text{Variance } (\sigma^2) = \Sigma\left(\frac{X - X}{n}\right)^2$$

$$\text{Standard Deviation (S.D. or } \sigma) = \sqrt{\Sigma \frac{(X - X)^2}{n}}$$

Indices of Variability

The above measurements use absolute values. Dispersion can also be shown relatively by indices of variability. These are:

Index of Variability

$$\frac{\text{Quartile deviation}}{\text{Median}} \times 100\%$$

Co-efficient of Variation

$$\frac{\text{Standard deviation}}{\text{Mean}} \times 100\%$$

Relative Variability

$$\frac{\text{Mean deviation}}{\bar{X}} \times 100\%$$

Pluvio-metric Co-efficient

$$cp = \frac{r}{R\frac{m}{365}}$$

where cp = pluvio-metric co-efficient

r = rainfall in the month

R = annual rainfall

m = number of days in that month

Normal Curve and Probability

In order to represent a set of data at least two parameters (characteristics) must be defined: first, the mean/average and second, deviation from the mean. Let us take a concrete example. The average yield of wheat per acre for a series of farms is 30 quintals and the standard deviation is 5 quintals. If the data in the series were symmetrically distributed about a central point (arithmetic mean), we will get a normal curve (Fig. 6.2).

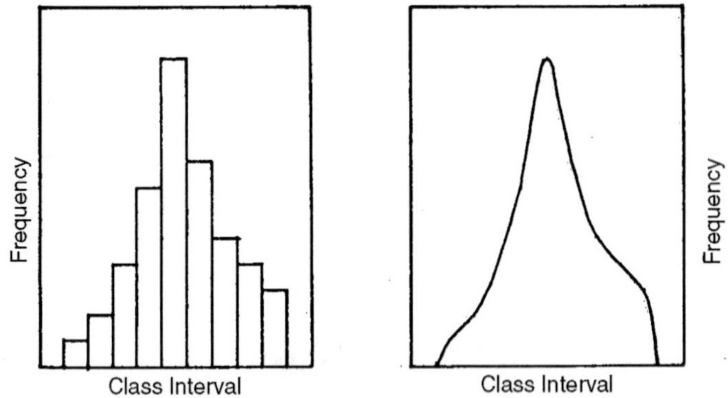

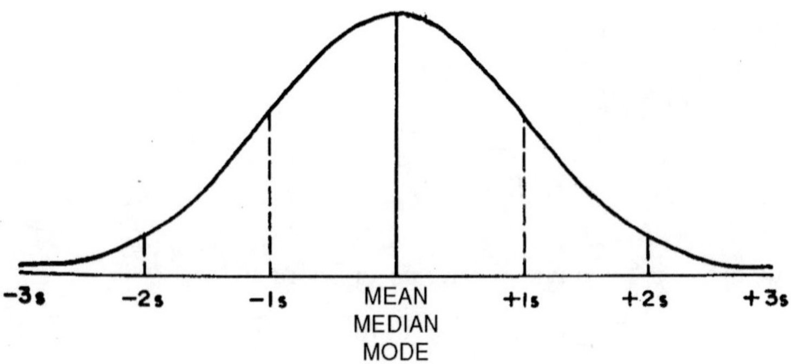

Fig. 6.2: A Normal Curve

In this figure, 68 per cent of the farms fall 1 standard deviation (SD) away from X (mean), i.e., 30 ± 5, and 95 per cent of the farms fall 2 SD away from the mean, and so on. More precisely:

68.30% of the occurrences lie within $\pm 1\sigma$

95.45% of the occurrences lie within $\pm 2\sigma$

99.7% of the occurrences lie within $\pm 3\sigma$

99.99% of the occurrences lie within $\pm 4\sigma$

Normal distribution of data is, however, not a common occurrence. Often they are asymmetrically distributed. In the case of symmetrical distribution, mean, median and mode are the same, but in an asymmetrical distribution, they are different. Asymmetry is marked with positive or negative skewness. In a positively skewed curve, mean exceeds the mode, and in a negatively skewed curve, mode exceeds the mean.

Degree of skewness can be expressed as co-efficient of skewness:

$$Skp = \frac{3\left(\bar{X} - \text{median}\right)}{SD}$$

where Skp = Co-efficient of skewness

X = Mean

SD = Standard deviation

Higher value means more skewness.

It does not, however, mean that all asymmetrical distributions produce curves of the same shape, i.e., all asymmetrical curves are not normal. Departure of an asymmetrical curve from the normal is called *kurtosis;* if it is too tapering, it is called *leptokurtic*; if too flat, it is called *plati-kurtic*; but if it is in-between and occupies a middle position, it is known as *meso-kurtic* (Fig. 6.3).

Linear Regression

It is a line describing the relationship between any two variables and may be called "the line of average relationship". In fact there are two regression lines, one for Y on X and the other for X on Y. In the first instance, it is possible to predict the approximate value of Y, given a value for X and *vice versa* for the regression of X on Y.

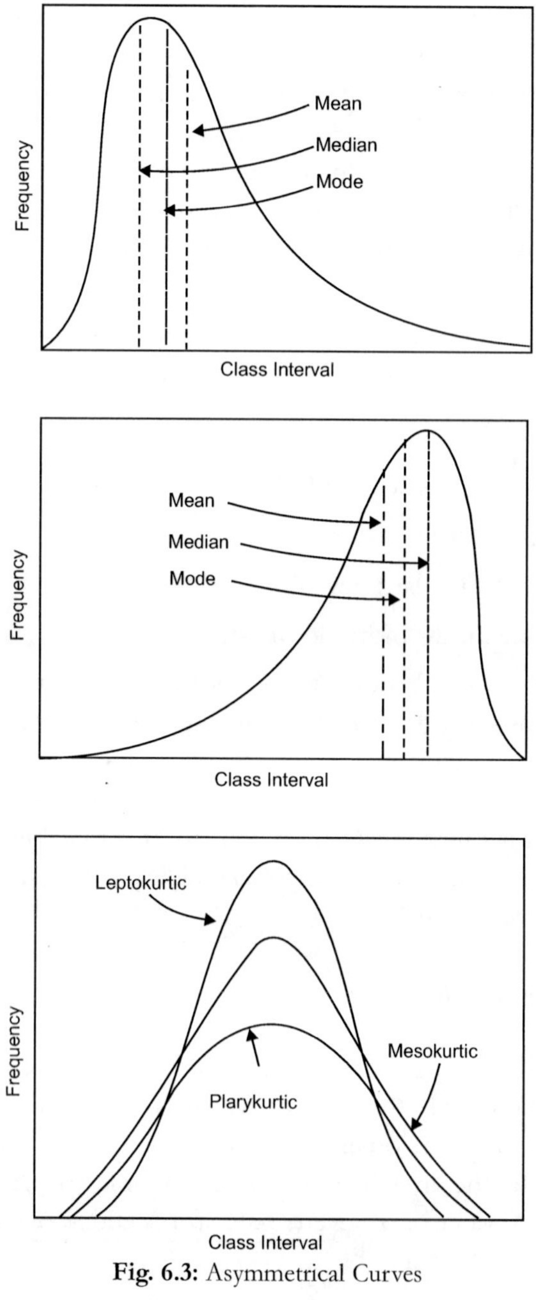

Fig. 6.3: Asymmetrical Curves

The equation for Y (unknown) on X (known) is

$$\left(Y-\bar{Y}\right) = r\frac{SDy}{SDx}\left(X-\bar{X}\right)$$

For X (unknown) and Y (known) the expression is

$$\left(X-\bar{X}\right) = r\frac{SDx}{SDy}\left(Y-\bar{Y}\right)$$

The regression equation of Y on X for the data referring to the employments and sales becomes

$$Y - 485 = 0.85 \times \frac{265.8}{21.68}\left(X-50\right)$$

$$Y = 10.17, X = 23.50$$

Taking arbitrary values,

$$X = 10, Y = 78.20$$

$$X = 20, Y = 179.90$$

The regression line for Y on X can also be found out as–

$$X - 50 = 0.85 \times \frac{21.68}{265.8}\left(Y-485\right)$$

$$X = .08\ Y = 11.20$$

These values may be used to draw the regression lines on a scatter diagram (Fig. 6.4).

Correlation

So far, we discussed the characteristics of a given set of data pertaining to one variable, and the methods of analyzing and

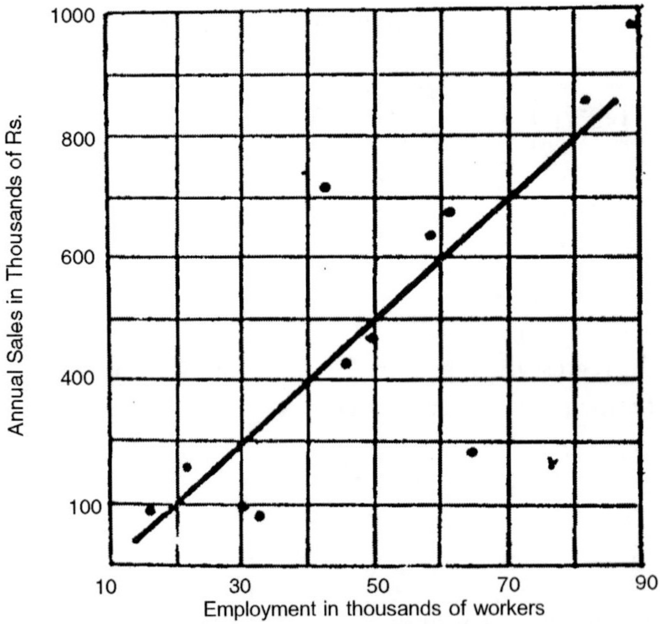

Fig. 6.4: A Regression Line

presenting it statistically. More often than not we have to compare two or more sets of data to find out the extent to which changes in one set of data trigger off changes in other set(s) of data. If the change in one set causes changes in other set(s), it means that individual items of the two sets of data co-exist either in time or space in such a way that the possibilities of interrelated changes cannot be ruled out. For such interrelated changes, we need indices that reflect the direction and/or magnitude in one set of data are associated with comparable changes in the other set(s). The index of Coefficient of Correlation is (*r*).

Co-efficient of Correlation

Coefficient of correlation (*r*) is one of the indices that quantify this association. It varies from –1 to +1. If it is –1 or nearer it, it means that the variables are negatively related to each other, i.e., when one increases, the other decreases proportionately. But if it is +1 or nearer to that, it means that they have perfect or high positive relationship. If it is 0, it means that they are not related to each other.

Let us take one specific example. Table 6.6 gives the employment figure as well as the sales in rupees in a given store.

Table 6.6: Number of People Employed and Annual Sales in a Store

Employment (workers in 1000s)	*Annual Sales (₹ in 1000s)*
22	250
31	200
90	850
82	850
43	710
65	280
59	630
16	180
61	670
46	420

The basic formula for the derivation of coefficient of correlation is,

$$r = \frac{\sum \frac{x}{SD_x} \cdot \frac{y}{SD_y}}{N} \quad \text{or} \quad \frac{\sum xy}{\sqrt{\sum x^2 \cdot y^2}}$$

where SD_x and SD_y = Standard deviations.

N = Number of items

x and y = Deviation values of X and Y respectively.

Table 6.7: Computation of Co-efficient of Correlation (r) (using the data given in Table 6.6)

X	Y	x = X–X	y = Y–Y	xy	X^2	Y^2
22	250	– 28	– 235	+6,580	784	55.225
31	200	– 19	– 285	+5,415	301	81.225
90	980	+ 40	+495	+19.800	1600	245,025
82	850	+32	+365	+11.680	1024	133,225
43	710	– 7	+225	–1.575	49	50.625
65	283	+ 15	– 205	–3.075	225	42.025
59	630	+ 19	+145	+10,370	1156	93.025
16	180	– 34	–305	+10,370	1156	93.025
61	670	+11	+185	+2.035	121	34.225
46	420	– 4	– 65	+260	121	4.225
35	190	– 15	+295	+4,425	225	87.025
50	460	0	– 25	0	0	625
600	5820	0	0	+57,220	5642	847,500
ΣX	ΣY	Σ_x	Σ_y	Σ_{xy}	Σ_x^2	Σ_y^2
X = 50	Y = 485			SD_X = 21.68	SD_Y = 2658	

$$\therefore \quad r = \frac{\Sigma xy}{\sqrt{\Sigma x^2 \cdot \Sigma y^2}} = \frac{57,220}{\sqrt{5612 \times 17,500}}$$

$$= +\ 0.83$$

The coefficient of + 0.83 implies that there is a high degree of positive correlation between employment and sales. Whenever employment increases, the sales also increase. In general the coefficients between + 0.5 and + 1 indicates a high degree of correlation and between –0.5 and + 0.5 indicates low level correlation. If it is zero, it means that the sets of data pertaining to *X* and *Y* change without affecting each other, i.e., there is no correlation between the two. The above said analysis of correlation coefficient is, however, not complete unless we determine the significance level of it. This can be done by conducting *t*-test. The formula for *t*-test is:

$$t = \frac{\sqrt{r^2(N-2)}}{1-r^2}$$

Rank Correlation

Rank Correlation measures the degree of association between two series. Its advantages are as follows:

(a) If the data are given, such as ranks, scores, etc., the degree of association can be found out by this method;

(b) It is quick, less laborious and useful where intensive study is not called for;

(c) It is helpful in correlating two sets of qualitative observations such as poor, fair, good, superior, etc.

Table 6.8 gives the data for calculating rank correlation between the size of labour force (*X*) and sales volume (*Y*):

Table 6.8: Labour Force and Sales Volume

Size of Labour Force	*Sales Volume*	*Rank of* X	*Rank of* Y
16	180	1	1
22	250	2	4
31	200	3	3
35	190	4	2
43	710	5	10
46	420	6	6
50	460	7	7
59	630	8	8
61	670	9	9
65	280	10	5
82	850	11	11
99	980	12	12

The formula for coefficient of rank correlation is

$$P = 1 - \frac{P = 1 - 6\sum D^2}{N\left(N^2 - 1\right)}$$

where P stands for the coefficient of rank correlation,

D stands for the difference between each pair of ranks,

N stands for Number of paired items, and

D stands for each pair of ranks. It can be found out by subtracting the rank of *Y* from the rank of its corresponding *X* (Table 6.9)

Table 6.9: Calculation of Difference in the Pair of Ranks

Rank of X	*Rank* of Y	*D*	D^2
1	1	0	0
2	4	– 2	4
3	3	0	0
4	2	2	4
5	10	– 5	25
6	6	0	0
7	7	0	0
8	8	0	0
9	9	0	0
10	5	5	25
11	11	0	0
12	12	0	0
		0	58

Now $$P = 1 - \frac{6(58)}{12(144-1)} = +\ 0.80$$

Sampling Errors in Correlation

If two samples of the same size are randomly selected from a given population, they would not give the same distribution on the scatter-diagram. The *r* values of the two would differ and none of them can be treated as perfectly reliable indication of the *r* obtained from the entire population. To determine the deviation of the *r* of a sample from the true *r* we have to calculate the standard error:

$$\sigma_r = \frac{1-r^2}{\sqrt{N}}$$

Suppose that the correlation (*r*) between *X* and *Y* is $r = .60$ for a given random sample of 100 cases, the standard error will be:

$$\frac{1-.6^2}{\sqrt{100}} = .064$$

This means that if *r* was similarly obtained they will fall into normal distribution with a standard deviation of approximately .064.

With the help of these methods, one can analyze the data and use them for statistical mapping. Only a few of the very elementary methods have been given in this chapter. Those interested in advanced work are referred to books on general statistics.

Multivariate Analysis

Multivariate statistics are employed for developing systems of classification, for group variates and to generate and test hypotheses. The concept underlying multivariate analysis that everything is linked to everything else; nothing stands alone in the world. In order to understand a phenomenon, we have to know what is there behind and underlying the phenomena we want to understand. This curiosity to know, leads us to multivariate analysis.

In multiple regression and analysis of variance, several variables are used; and a dependent variable is generally predicted or explained by means of independent variables and covariates. Then there are methods to find out interrelationships among the variable such as factor analysis, multidimensional scaling

(MDS) and cluster analysis. All these statistical techniques are discussed below.

Multiple Regression

Multiple Regression was first used by Pearson in 1908. It helps in finding out relationship between a number of independent variables and a dependent variable. For example, an agricultural extension worker may like to know why output of wheat per acre in different farms is not the same. Could it be because of poor quality of seeds, low input of fertilizers, or size of the farm? The question is how these variables relate to output of the farms.

In the natural and social science researches multiple regression procedures are very widely used particularly when one has to seek the best predictor of a phenomenon. In the above case, an extension officer wants to know the best predictors of high yields of wheat. An educational researcher may want to know the best predictors of success in high school. A psychologists may seek to know which personality variable best predicts social adjustment. Sociologists may want to find out which of the multiple social indicators best predict whether or not a new immigrant group will adapt and be absorbed into society. A geographer may try to know the indicators of development disparities.

As an example, let us take an independent variable X (*IQ* of students measured by a test) and one dependent variable Y (school achievement as reflected by average grade point – *GPA*). Each point in the scatter plot (Fig. 6.5) represents respective student's *IQ* and *GPA*.

The scatter plot is formed by an independent or X variable (IQ), and a dependent or Y variable (GPA). Each point in the plot represents one student's IQ and GPA. The Y variable can

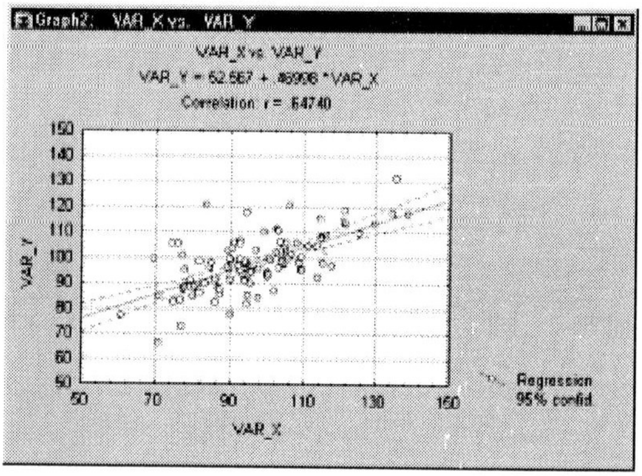

Fig. 6.5: Scatter Plot of a Simple Case of Multiple Regression

be expressed in terms of a constant (*a*) and a slope (*b*) times the *X* variable, i.e., $Y = a + b/X$. The constant is also referred to as the *intercept*, and the slope as the *regression coefficient* or *B coefficient.* The GPA may be predicted as $1 + .02/IQ$. Thus, if a student has an *IQ* of 130 we can get his/her GPA to be 3.6 (since, $1 + .02/130 = 3.6$).

In the multivariate case, there is more than one independent variable hence the regression line is not visualized in the two dimensional space. But the computational process is similar and easy. Suppose that there are three independent/predictor variables: IQ, Motivation, and Self-discipline. Now we construct a linear equation containing all those variables. It will take the following form:

$$Y = a + b_1/X_1 + b_2/X_2 + \ldots + b_p/X_p.$$

In this case the regression coefficients or *B* coefficients, represent the contributions of each of the three independent variables to the prediction of the dependent variable.

Table 6.10 gives the data on agricultural productivity and its determinants for Tamil Nadu districts. We have to calculate the coefficient of correlation between agricultural productivity measured in rupees and the factors influencing/determining it.

Table 6.10: Agricultural Productivity and its Determinants (Tamil Nadu 1972-75)

S. No.	Districts	y	x_1	x_2	x_3	x_4	x_5	x_6
1.	Chingleput	2300	135.26	68.03	60.63	5.41	9.14	87.50
2.	South Arcot	2682	121.82	56.64	52.15	5.02	6.97	84.75
3.	North Arcot	2297	128.68	53.57	36.31	5.43	6.19	69.47
4.	Salem & Dharmapuri	1556	118.64	27.34	22.07	3.82	5.10	65.68
5.	Coimbatore	2028	117.07	43.42	46.20	4.93	1.46	55.72
6.	Tiruchirapalli	1593	111.74	40.04	41.40	2.41	8.15	61.40
7.	Thanjavur	2023	161.28	71.06	53.17	1.71	0.92	87.04
8.	Madurai	1784	113.14	41.47	33.81	2.92	0.43	70.10
9.	Ramanathapuram	1226	103.16	38.76	15.98	1.22	5.32	59.46
10.	Tirunelveli	1794	120.18	44.40	25.59	2.02	9.35	80.94
11.	Nilgiris	3517	100.11	0.38	45.22	0.86	3.29	150.60
12.	Kanya Kumari	2364	144.70	50.57	33.44	0.42	3.97	188.78

Y = Agricultural Productivity per ha in rupees
X_1 = Intensity of cropping
X_2 = Proportion of GOA to GCA
X_3 = Consumption of fertilizer per 1000 ha
X_4 = Mechanisation index
X_5 = Proportion of area under non-food crops
X_6 = Mean annual rainfall in cms

Source: Parimala, G.; *Levels of Agricultural Development in Tamil Nadu: A Talukawise Study,* M Phil Dissertation Submitted in CSRD, JNU.

As a first step, a multiple correlation matrix like the one given in Table 6.11 is obtained.

Table 6.11: Multiple Correlation Matrix

	Y	X_1	X_2	X_3	X_4	X_5	X_6
Y	1.000						
X_1	0.544	1.00					
X_2	0.644	0.767	1.00				
X_3	0.690	0.527	0.793	1.00			
X_4	0.521	– 0.150	0.221	0.575	1.00		
X_5	0.110	– 0.509	– 0.425	– 0.391	- 0.330	1.00	
X_6	0.574	0.725	0.449	0.207	– 0.234	– 0.260	1.00

The correlation co-efficient values in Table 6.11 show the mutual inter-correlation between the dependent variable and independent variables. Let us now interpret this computer created matrix. We notice that X_1 has high positive correlation (+0.767) with X_2, and X_3 has still higher positive correlation (+0.793) with X_2. It happens if the independent variables are not so independent. This is known as multi-collinearity. In the present case, this has occurred because X_3 (irrigation) has high correlation with cropping intensity (X_1).

The correlation matrix provides the base for further step-wise regression. Table 6.12 presents the results of this regression exercise.

Table 6.12: Order of the Variables added in the Step-wise Regression.

Steps	*Included variable*	*R*	*R^2 x 100*	*Increase in R^2 × 100*	*Steward error*	*R*	*R^2 × 100*	*Increase in R^2 × 100*
I	x_3	0.690	47.7		325.010	0.690	47.7	
II	x_3x_6	0.819	67.1	19.4	288.009	0.797	63.5	15.8
III	$x_3x_6x_5$	0.965	93.2	26.1	148.652	0.956	91.3	27.8
IV	$x_3x_6x_5x_2$	0.966	93.4	0.2	169.313	0.951	90.4	–0.9
V	$x_3x_6x_5x_2x_4$	0.967	93.6	0.2	196.781	0.945	89.3	–0.1
VI	$x_3x_6x_5x_2x_4x_1$	0.968	93.6	0.0	240.921	0.934	87.2	–2.1

In the above exercise, fertilizer enters in the first step. All the independent variables together explain 93.6 per cent of the variations in agriculture productivity in Tamil Nadu. The variables are more important in explaining the variations only up to the third step. R^2 also starts decreasing as X_2 enters the fourth step. Thus, as the exercise proceeds the explanatory power of independent variables increases but the significance level decreases.

Once the problem of multi-collinearity is detected, further processing of the data can be done to eliminate this problem.

Much depends on the usage of this technique in relevant research areas.

In general, the degree to which two or more independent variables (*X*) are related to the dependent variable (*Y*) is expressed in the correlation coefficient R *which in the case of multiple regression* can assume values between 0 and 1. To interpret the direction of the relationship between the variables, the plus or minus signs of the regression or *B* coefficients are kept in view. If a *B* coefficient is positive, then the relationship of this variable with the dependent variable is positive (e.g., the greater the IQ, the better the grade point average); if the *B* coefficient is negative then the relationship is negative (e.g., the lower the class size, the better the average test scores). A 0 coefficient points to the absence of any relationship between the variables.

Analysis of Variance (ANOVA)

An ANOVA is used to find out differences between groups on a given variable. For example, a teacher may be interested in finding out if the class performance of his students is related to final grade of students or not. First, he would divide the students according to their grades and then see if performance is different across the grades.

The simplest version of ANOVA is one-way between groups model. Here, it is only the final grade that is being used to define the groups. A two-way between groups ANOVA is used to look at complex groupings. For example, the grades by class performance analysis could be extended to find out the differences in the performance of students from two different States of India.

Procedure for calculating ANOVA, using the data pertaining to the performance of the students is as follows:

1. *Step I:* Calculate the Group Mean, i.e., the mean for each of the final grading groups on the class performance data.
2. *Step II*: Calculate the Overall Mean, i.e., the mean for all the groups combined.
3. *Step III*: Calculate Within Group Variation, i.e., total deviation of each individual's score within each group from the Group Mean.
4. *Step IV*: Calculate Between Group Variation, i.e., the deviation of each Group Mean from the Overall Mean.
5. *Step V*: Produce the F statistic which is the ratio Between Group Variation to the Within Group Variation.

If the Between Group Variation is significantly greater than the Within Group Variation, then it is likely that there is a statistically significant difference between the groups.

Chi Square (χ^2)

Chi is a Greek letter pronounced as 'kye'. It is a non-parametric statistical technique expressed as χ^2. It is used to determine whether a distribution of observed frequencies is the same as theoretically expected or not. The frequencies may be expressed in nominal (categorical) or ordinal mode but they should not be expressed as percentages, ratios, means and variances.

Chi square is the sum of the squared difference between observed (*o*) and the expected (*e*) figures (or the deviation, *d*), divided by the expected data. To put in the form of a formula:

$$\chi^2 = \frac{(0-e)^2}{e}$$

where χ^2 is the chi square statistic, *o* is the observed frequency and *e* is the expected frequency.

Data used in a chi square analysis should satisfy following conditions:

1. They should be randomly drawn from the population,
2. They should be reported in raw counts of frequency,
3. Their measured variables must be independent,
4. Their observed frequencies should not be too small, and
5. The values of independent and dependent variables must be mutually exclusive.

There are two types of χ^2 test:

1. Chi square test for goodness of fit; it compares expected and observed frequencies to determine how well the predictions fit the data; and
2. Chi square test for independence; it compares two sets of categories to determine how differently the groups are distributed among the categories.

Chi Square Test for Goodness of Fit

If we toss a coin 100 times, the outcome would generally be 50 heads and 50 tails. But if the outcome is 47 heads and 53 tails, it may be because the coin is defective or because of a chance. To test it, we first formulate our hypothesis which, may be stated in one of the following two forms:

1. *Null hypothesis*: The coin is fair
2. *Alternate hypothesis*: The coin is biased

distributed among the people, 45 degree line would become the Lorentz Curve. If all the income is owned by just one person, the Lorentz Curve would be the baseline. Nearer the Lorentz Curve is the Line of Equality, lesser the inequality.

Gini Coefficient

Gini Coefficient was formulated by Italian statistician Corrado Gini in 1912. It is closely related to Lorentz Curve and shows how far a given variable deviates from equal distribution. Gini coefficient is thus the ratio of the area that lies between the line of equality and the Lorentz Curve (marked 'A' in the figure) over the total area under the line of equality (marked 'A' and 'B' in the figure); i.e.

$$G = A/(A + B).$$

The Gini Coefficient ranges from 0 to 1; at times it is multiplied by 100 to range between 0 and 100. Lower the Gini coefficient more equal the distribution, and higher the Gini coefficient more unequal the distribution. Thus, Gini = 0 means complete equality, i.e., every person receives the same income, and Gini = 1 means complete inequality, i.e., a single person receives 100 per cent of the total income and the remaining people receive none.

Given a Lorentz Curve, G can be calculated mathematically too. Since $A + B = 0.5$, the Gini index, $G = A/(0.5) = 2A =$ 1–2 B. If the Lorentz Curve is represented by the function $Y = L(X)$, the value of B can be found with integration and:

$$G = 1-2\int_0^1 L(X)dX$$

$$G = \frac{1}{n}\left(n+1-2\left(\frac{\sum_{i=1}^{n}(n+1-i)y_i}{\sum_{i=1}^{n}y_i}\right)\right)$$

$$G = 1-\frac{\sum_{i=1}^{n}f(y_i)(S_{i-1}+S_i)}{S_n}$$

While Gini-coefficient is a very commonly used measure of inequality, it has certain disadvantages too. Its main advantage is that it is a simple measure of inequality and can be easily interpreted. It measures inequality by means of a ratio analysis, rather than a variable that does not represent most of the population, such as per capita income or GDP. It can be used to compare income distributions across different components of the population (like urban and rural) as well as countries. It can be used to indicate how the distribution of income has changed over a period of time, thus it is possible to see if inequality is increasing or decreasing.

Gini-coefficient suffers from certain disadvantages too. It does not tell why the inequality in income. It does not tell the level of the economy. Both rich and poor countries can have the same *G*. It does not express regional variations. The Lorentz Curve may understate the actual amount of inequality if richer households are able to use income more efficiently than lower income households or *vice versa*. It measures income rather than wealth. As with other inequality coefficients, the Gini coefficient is influenced by the granularity of the measurements. It is not a measure of egalitarianism; it is only a measure of income dispersion. The Gini coefficient is a point-estimate of equality at a certain time; hence it ignores life-span changes in income. It does not take into account the benefits people get from the government in terms of subsidized food, education, health facilities, etc.

Pareto Distribution

Named after the famous Swiss economist/sociologist Wilfredo Pareto, Pareto distribution is a power law probability distribution found in a large number of real-world situations. The power-law implies that large occurrences are rare while the small occurrences are extremely common. This regularity or 'law' is sometimes also referred to as Zipf or Bradford distribution. It explains why many manmade and natural phenomena, including wealth, incomes, city sizes, word frequencies, and earthquake magnitudes follow a power-law distribution.

While studying family income distribution in Switzerland, Pareto discovered that there were more families with a low income than families with a large income, and that these distributions followed a very smooth pattern. Seeing the regularity of this phenomenon, larger portion of the wealth of any society is owned by a smaller pattern of wealth distribution, Pareto converted it into a principle which is often referred to as '80-20 rule' or Pareto principle, which says that 20 per cent of the people control 80 per cent of the wealth. It further says that the fraction of population (80%) that owns a small amount of wealth (20%) per person decreases steadily as total wealth increases. In other words, less developed an economy more unevenly distributed is the wealth of a nation. This is the ground on which economists contend that rapid economic growth would lead to better distribution of wealth.

If we draw a Probability Density Function (PDF) graph of the population $f(x)$, the probability, or fraction of $f(x)$ owning a small amount of wealth per head, is high. As wealth increases, the probability or fraction of population owing small amount of wealth, decreases as wealth increases.

Mathematically, the Straight Line part of the graph can be expressed as:

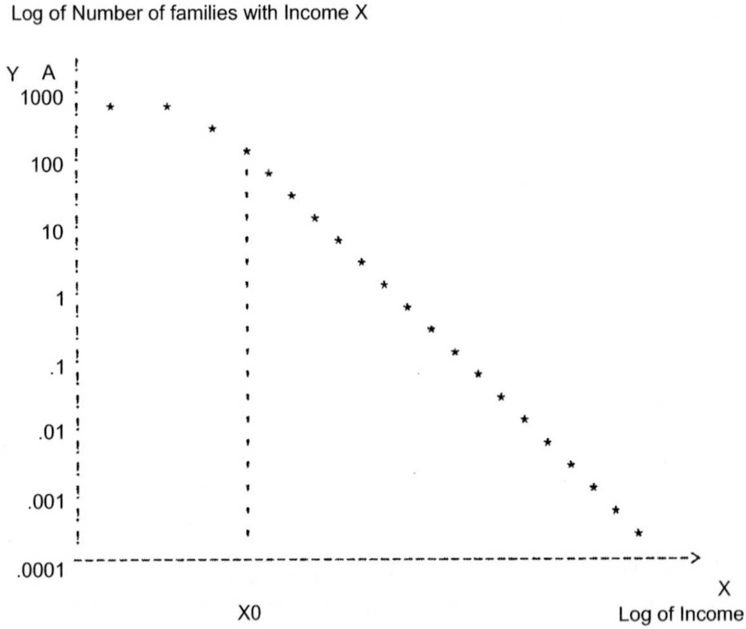

Fig. 6.7: Pareto Distrbution

$$Y = A\,X + B$$

where,

X is the logarithm of the income level x and

Y is the logarithm of the number of people having an income x

The Pareto distribution, however, fails to give a good fit for the lower end of the size spectrum. It was admitted by Pareto himself that his principle was valid only above a minimum size X_0.

References

Abelson, R.P. (1995), *Statistics as Principled Argument,* NJ: Lawrence Erlbaum Associates.

Argyrous, G. (2000), *Statistics for Social and Health Research,*(with a guide to SPSS), London: Sage Publications.

Best, J. (2004), *More Damned Lies and Statistics: How Numbers Confuse Public Issues.* CA: University of California Press.

Brown, F.L., Amos, J.R., & Mink, O.G. (1995), *Statistical Concepts—A Basic Program,* NY: HarperCollins College Publishers.

Craft, J.L. (1990*), Statistics and Data Analysis for Social Workers,* 2nd Edition, Itasca, IL: F.E. Peacock Publishers

Diamond, I. & Jefferies, J. (2001), *Beginning Statistics. An Introduction for Social Scientists,* CA: Sage Publications.

Foster, J.J. (2001), *Data Analysis Using SPSS for Windows Versions 8 to 10: A Beginner's Guide,* CA: Sage Publications.

Freed, M.N.; Ryan, J.M.; & Kess, R.K. (1991), *Handbook of Statistical Procedures and Their Computer Applications to Education and the Behavioural Sciences,* New York: American Council on Education, Macmillan Publishing Company.

Gigerenzer, G. (2002), *Calculated Risks: How To Know When Numbers Deceive You,* New York: Simon & Shuster MacMillan Co.

Graham, A. (2003), *Teach Yourself Statistics,* New York: McGraw Hill.

Jaisingh, L. (2000), *Statistics for the Utterly Confused,* New York: McGraw Hill.

Kaplan M. and Kaplan, E. (2006). *Chances Are… Adventures in Probability,* New York: Penguin/Viking Group.

Langley, R. (1970), *Practical Statistics,* New York: Dover Books.

Levitt, Steven D. & Dubner, Stephen J. (2005), *Freakonomics. A Rogue Economist Explores the Hidden Side of Everything.* New York: Harper Collins Publishers.

Mlodinow, L. (2008), *The Drunkard's Walk. How Randomness Rules Our Lives* New York: Vintage Books.

Moore, D.S. (1991), *Statistics Concepts and Controversies,* 3rd Edition. New York: WH Freeman & Co.

matter and the personality of the writer. Three methods for organizing facts and ideas for scientific writing are suggested. (1) The separate card method utilizes a card for each fact and idea. On a distinguishable set of cards are listed the main structural parts of a manuscript such as introduction, purpose, procedure, etc. Then the fact cards are sorted and placed in their appropriate category. With this material in front of the writer the first draft is merely a process of connecting the facts and ideas; (2) For the more experienced writer there is the total recall method. Mentally, the prospective author recalls in general terms what he was trying to find out, what he did, and why, and when. From this mental outline he writes down a series of general statements. (a) I asked the question…, (b) To find an answer, I adopted the method of…, (c) Using this method I obtained the following observations…, (d) From these data I conclude…. The first draft is written directly from this outline. In this method the emphasis is placed on thinking through the entire report in order to assemble logically the facts and ideas; (3) Called the relaxed method, the manuscript itself, plus the author's original unformalized plan, serves as the outline. In practice, this is a process of writing a few paragraphs, stopping for a period of time; upon beginning writing again, the writer revises the text and composes a new until he has completed the report. This method is recommended only for the experienced writer.

The preliminary outline should be planned carefully in order to ensure that all facts are considered logically. It is easier to shift sections in an outline than to shift paragraphs in the written copy.

Drafting the Manuscript

The first draft is written directly from the outline. Begin the writing in a systematic manner with a relaxed frame of mind. Write rapidly; if you have trouble, leave a blank for words that do not come readily to mind. In addition, write only on alternate lines, thus leaving room for later changes. While writing, if you get tired or bored, take a break. You should always try to finish a given segment at one sitting because a break in your train of thought might mean losing a good idea. Finally, leave time in your schedule for putting your completed first draft aside for at least a day before beginning to revise it. This will enable you to take a more critical view of it.

When writing the first draft certain aspects should be covered in the introduction, body, and conclusions of the manuscript. The introduction should include enough of the history of the problem to show how the new data relate to earlier work or to the science in general. If the author can sketch in the relevant points of earlier studies, even briefly, he will help both the beginner in his own field and the scientist in a related field. The introduction should point out the basic assumptions, if any. underlying the arguments. Many reports, especially those of an interpretative or theoretical nature, are based on certain hypotheses that may seem to the author to be implicit in the discussion. Nevertheless, he should state them clearly and concisely, for the benefit of less sophisticated readers.

The body of any piece of writing is the meat of a writer's ideas. Here you give all your facts and substantiate them. You develop your major and minor points and tie them together into a clearly comprehensible whole. The Case with which you develop your subject in the body of your text depends upon the adequacy of your research, prior thought and outline. Gathering a multiplicity of details before you begin to write and then pruning them down to essentials is a better practice for most of us than gathering a sparse quantity of details and trying to build them up to a tightly woven argument or description. Above all, the body of the exposition should leave no gaps in your reasoning. Here is where you test every statement and substantiate it by detailed explanations or proof.

The conclusion may be a brief restatement of the principal ideas covered in the paper; it may be a restatement of the purpose of a described object; in the research paper it may be a statement of conclusions reached through the research study. The conclusion may also include a prophecy, such as, "Future research may prove that…" or "A later study will be attempted to learn whether the relationship between…." Whatever form the conclusion takes, it should so summarize the main idea of the study that it sharpens and solidifies that idea in the mind of the reader.

Writing for the Report

Before undertaking writing, it is essential to have in mind the educational level of the reader to whom it is addressed, as this will govern the whole approach to the style and treatment of the material. Writing, in essence, is a conversation between people, not a monologue into the void. The writer sets down his comments and the reader answers by his acceptance or rejection of the ideas. 'The golden rule in scientific writing is, therefore, to put yourself constantly in the place of the reader."[5] If there are no readers, the labour of writing is wasted and it is, therefore, in the writer's own interest to secure and hold the reader's attention.

Style

The selection of words, the choice of sentence structure, the ideas to be expressed, the point of view, the audience addressed, all help to form the style of a composition. What are the essentials of a scientific style? It is generally agreed that the qualities of greatest importance in a good scientific style are clarity, precision, conciseness, directness and objectivity.

Clarity and precision are to a great degree interdependent. Clarity results when the writer is successful in making his communication understandable to the reader. Precision represents rather the attainment of an exact correspondence between the matter to be conveyed and its verbal expressions.

Writing that is concise—that expresses its meaning in the fewest possible words—saves the time and energy of the reader and contributes to readability. Directness also serves these ends and facilitates communication through the avoidance of circumlocutions and awkward inversions and of excessively numerous "there is" and "it is" constructions in which the appearance of the subject is delayed. In general, directness is the foe of verbiage, which impedes a simple, straightforward approach.

It is expected that the scientist's style should reflect the objectivity of his attitude toward the problems he investigates and towards his results. This emphasis on objectivity as a quality of scientific style implies that in subordinating subjective considerations, scientific style should be more formal and more impersonal than is prose style in general.

Two factors work against the scientist in his writing. The journals plead for brevity, and custom urges him to write impersonally. The style of much of the resulting prose reflects a writer under restraint.

Here is an example:

> In order for us to understand the details of the history of our attempts to interpret the complicated phenomenon of heat in its evolution from the now

> extinct caloric concept to the accepted kinetic theory, there are several alternative approaches all of which we must pursue if we are to understand the nature of the phenomenon.[6]

The style of this long, complex sentence, carrying its burden of unnecessary words, almost buries the author's thought. With enough patience, however, a reader can finally recover it:

> Heat is a complicated phenomenon. Physicists have now discarded the idea of a caloric fluid and have generally adopted the kinetic theory. A review of the earlier concepts, however, will help us to understand the nature of heat.[7]

The original version was hard to understand, not because of the grammar but because of the style.

A more or less deformed style inevitably develops when a writer accepts the convention that the scientist must write impersonally. Avoiding the first person does not necessarily produce grammatical mistakes, of course, but it does encourage indirect statements. In addition, the need to use passive verbs increases the probability of errors in grammar. Passive verbs start long trains of prepositional phrases; they foster circumlocution; and they encourage vagueness. A writer will almost automatically improve his style if he shifts from passive to active construction.

In general, short, simple sentences make the clearest exposition. A very long sentence strains the reader to understand what it says. Sometimes a good explanation requires a long sentence; the author should then help the reader as much as possible. The predicate should follow closely to the subject, and modifying clauses should appear close to the words they modify. The experienced writer will vary the length of his sentences as a short sentence placed among longer complex structures provides emphasis as well as relief.

Thus, to achieve a good style in scientific writing an author needs only a few principles; write simply, avoid long sentences, choose plain words, and use active voice.

Functional English and its Use

The style for presenting facts and instructions is known to scientific writers as functional English. Its mood, person, and tense may be varied to suit particular documents, but it remains essentially the presentation of exact reasoning with mathematical precision. Sentences are confined to the function they are required to serve. They deal with a single topic and give their message in crisp, direct phraseology.

Chief among the hazards confronting the scientist preparing a manuscript is his unconscious blunders in English. The majority of grammatical errors are caused by carelessness in writing and can usually be found by the writer when he checks his first draft. Most common errors are likely to be— (1) faulty agreement; (2) incomplete constructions; (3) dangling constructions. Faulty agreement is the incorrect agreement of verbs with their subjects and of pronouns with their antecedents. Two types of incomplete constructions are more common than the sentence fragment—(a) When two verbs have the same subject or object, an error may occur in the omission of a necessary verb auxiliary. Such omission causes fragmentary construction within the sentence; (b) Comparisons—a sentence is not complete unless all comparisons and implied comparisons are expressed and proper conjunctions used. A common error is to omit the second part of a comparison or to omit a word needed to make a sentence of comparison grammatically correct; (3) Dangling constructions—the participle, the gender, the noun,

helpful advice, as a rule, from sympathetic and informed colleagues.

Evaluate the conclusions with special care. Have you adequately discussed the evidence you presented earlier? Have you pointed out how the evidence relates to your original problem? Have you stated your conclusions in definite terms? The reader should be able to understand exactly what this particular investigation accomplishes and what it means.

With the manuscript written and revised, the main task has been completed. One important consideration is the selection of a title. The title selected should be brief and as a rule it should not occupy more than one printed line. The title should indicate the subject of the manuscript but should not attempt to summarize the content. A good, brief title gives a general rather than a detailed description of the contents.

The summary consists of few paragraphs stating succinctly the problem or subject and the main conclusions reached by the writer. It provides a predigested abridgement of report so that the busy reader can tell at a glance whether the subject is one that interests him. More than that, the summary is a discipline for the writer, forcing him to test his thesis to see if it has one central idea or conclusion that can be stated in capsule form.

The author alone must decide how many drafts of a manuscript are enough. The complexity of the material as well as the care in writing will determine when one can stop revising and pronounce the most recent draft the last.

Format for Scientific Reporting

Before starting the writing task the researcher should see that the following steps have been taken:

1. Outline is completed and if needed revised;
2. Notes written on the scratch sheets are properly filed under various sections of the outline file; and
3. Bibliography is alphabetized in the alphabetic Index Cards File.

If these steps have been taken the remaining thinking and writing tasks will seem easy.

After its completion a research report will have three main divisions. These are:

1. The preliminaries;
2. The text; and
3. The reference materials.

The Preliminaries

The Title and Half-Title Page

The first element of the preliminaries is the title page. A title page should indicate the title of the report, institution or organization which published it, the name of the author/editor and the time and place of publication. In what order should all these come depends on individual taste, but in most cases the date and place of publication come last.

The Title page may be followed by a Half-Title page. The Half-Title page should ordinarily give more information about the Title, the writer and the publisher. For example, it may also give the Sub-Title if any and the designation and qualification of the writer. This page should be paginated as the first page of the preliminaries indicated by small Roman numbers but the page number should not appear on it.

Preface and Acknowledgement

The Half-Title page is followed by a preface. A Preface includes such matters as the writer's reasons for conducting the research, and the scheme or programme under which the study was conducted. A Preface is also a suitable place to mention the assistance given by the organizations or individuals in the process of research. If a student does not wish to mention anything except the assistance he received, then he may do away with the preface and replace it by "Acknowledgement".

Table of Contents

After Preface comes the "Table of Contents". A Table of Contents shows the main headings including the chapter headings in capital letters. The chapter heading is preceded by chapter number in capital Roman numerals. On the left hand side of the page the word "chapter" in small letters is typed above the column of chapter numbers and on the right hand side the word "page" above the column of page numbers. For illustration see the Table of Contents of this handbook.

The chapters in the text are usually divided into sub-headings of first, second or sometimes even third orders. Whether all sub-headings should appear in the Table of Contents or not will have to be decided by the writer himself. If they are given, the following should be the system. The sub-headings of the first order are typed in capital and small letters. The first letter of the first and the last words together with that of all nouns, pronouns, adjectives, adverbs and verbs should be capitalised. The sub-headings of the second order should contain only the first letter of the first word capital and while that of the third order should not have any capital letters unless, of course, they happen to be proper nouns or proper adjectives. Each author should develop his own style.

The spacing between the chapter headings should be double. It should also be double between the chapter heading and the sub-headings of the first order. The spacing between the sub-headings should be single.

At times the sub-headings are also numbered. In the case of numbering, the sub-headings of the first order should be numbered in capital letters, i.e., A – Z, those of the second order in International numerals, i.e., 1, 2, 3,... those of the third order in small letters, i.e., *a–z*, and those of the fourth order in small Roman numbers i, ii, iii....

The Table of Contents should incorporate all sections of the report including the preliminaries and the reference materials. The preliminaries, however, are paginated in small Roman numerals.

List of Tables and Illustrations

Table of Contents is followed by the List of Tables which shows the table numbers in Indian or Roman numerals and the titles in capital and small letters. In order to avoid repetition, the word "table" in small letters is typed above the column of table numbers, and the word "page" above the column of page numbers, as in the case of table of contents.

The 'List of Illustrations' is placed after the List of Tables. It is advisable to designate all illustrations as figures and to number them in international numerals. The title of the figure in the list of illustrations should be the same as it appears with the figure. It can be shortened only in very exceptional cases. (for illustration see the list of illustrations in this handbook).

With the List of Illustrations, the preliminary part of the report is over and the next part, i.e., the text begins.

The Text

Chapters and Sub-Headings

The text of a paper begins with an "INTRODUCTION". An introduction can be the first chapter of the report or if it is short, it may be referred to as "Introduction" without chapter number.

Ordinarily an "Introduction" contains the objectives, methods of research, and the organizational structure of the report. Other chapters follow the introduction.

Introduction as well as the other chapters can be divided by sub-headings of various orders as pointed out earlier. The problem naturally arises as to what should be the location of various orders of sub-headings in the text. Supposing that three orders are used, the following scheme will be most appropriate.

Centre heading, *underlined;*

Side heading, *underlined;*

Paragraph heading, *underlined.*

If it is required to have as many as six orders of sub-headings the following system may be used:

Centred heading, *underlined;*

Centred heading, *not underlined;*

Side heading, *underlined;*

Side heading, *not underlined;*

Paragraph heading, *underlined;*

Paragraph heading, *not underlined.*

The paragraph heading should be followed by a colon and a dash. The system of using the capital and small letters is the same as discussed earlier under "Table of Contents". The last chapter of the text should be the "Summary and Conclusions" or only "Summary."

Quotations

Wherever, it is necessary to quote a passage or a verse from a publication, it can be put in the text. As far as possible the quotation should correspond with the original in wording, spelling and punctuation.

If the quotation is a small one, i.e., a sentence or two, it may be incorporated into the text of the report and enclosed in quotation marks. Wherever a quotation is incorporated within the text, one should see that it fits in the sentence grammatically. But if it is a long one containing more than two sentences, it should be put separately from the text in single spacing. It should be located four spaces to the left of the left hand margin. In this case it is not necessary to put quotation marks.

At times one comes across such quotable passages which contain certain sentences which are irrelevant to the subject. In such cases the authors are free to delete the irrelevant portions. This is done by substituting each of those portions by three dots. This process is called elipsis. If after the elipsis there is a full stop, the number of dots will be four. In case a whole paragraph or a line or more in a verse are omitted, the elipsis should be shown by a full line of spaced dots.

It sometimes so happens that a quotation contains an error. If it is given in a text without any warning, the reader may feel

T.C. Chamberlin and R.D. Salisbury, *Geology,* Vol. I, *Geologic Processes and Their Results,* (IInd ed., rev.; New York; Henry Holt & Co., 1969), p. 155.

For articles:

The form of footnotes for articles published in professional periodicals is different from that for the books. The author's name is given in the normal order, i.e., the initials are followed by the family name. The next item is the title of the articles within double quotation marks. The title is followed by the name of the periodical (underlined). The volume number, the month and the year of publication and the page numbers referred to are given after the name of the periodical. The basic form looks as follows:

R.S. Ecksus, "Factor Proportions in Underdeveloped Countries", *American Economic Review,* XLV (Sept. 1955), pp. 539-65.

William E. Moore, "The Social Framework of Economic Development", in *Tradition, Values and Socio-Economic Development,* edited by R. Braibanti and J. Spengler (Durham: Duke University Press, 1961), p. 69.

If there are more than three writers, the name of the first writer followed by the abbreviation *et al.,* (underlined) should be given. If the writer happens to be an editor and not an author, the abbreviation (ed.,) in parenthesis should be put after his name. If the work has been translated by someone, the abbreviation 'trans' followed by the name of the translator should appear after the title of the work.

If a publication belongs to a series, it may be footnoted as follows:

> Marcel J. De Meirleir, *Manufactural Occupance in the West Central Areas of Chicago,* Department of Geography Research Paper No. 11 (Chicago: Chicago University Press, 1950), p. 11.
>
> William Burge, *Theoretical Geography,* Lund Studies in Geography, Series C. General and Mathematical Geography, No. 1 (Lund: Royal University of Lund, Sweden, 1962), p. 8.

If the publication happens to be a report without an author, the name of the author may be omitted. The rest of the form stands. If it is a newspaper, only the name of the paper followed by the date and year of publication together with the page number referred to should be given.

> *Indian Express* (Bangalore), August 29, 1965, p. 5.

If the reference is unpublished such as a dissertation the citation should appear as follows:

> R.P. Misra, "Agricultural Development in a Traditional Society — A Theoretical and Empirical Analysis of the Processes of Agricultural Development and Change in Lancaster Country, Pennsylvania" (Unpublished Ph.D., Dissertation, Department of Geography, University of Maryland, College Park, Md., U.S.A., 1964), pp. ...

If a reference cited before has to be cited again, the following system should be adopted: (1) If the references to the same work follow each other without any other intervening reference, even though separated by several pages, the reference in question should not be repeated. Instead the abbreviation "*ibid.*" should be used. It is, however, not permissible to use '*ibid.*' if the work cited is different although the author is the same; (2) But in case the second reference to the same work is intervened by other references, the last name of the author together with the page number under reference should be noted. There is no need to repeat the full form of the footnote.

Tables and Illustrations

Tables: Usually a table is put immediately after it is first mentioned in the text. But in case it cannot be accommodated within the space left out in the page, it should be placed in the following page. The table number in international numerals must be put at its appropriate place in the text to indicate the exact position to which it belongs. If the table is too wide to be accommodated length-wise in a page, it can be put broad-side.

The caption of the table should be preceded by the word "TABLE" in capital letters and table number in international numerals. A colon is placed after the table number. The caption of a table should be centred in the page by leaving five to seven spaces on both sides of the caption (see *Appendix A).*

There are, of course, several styles of writing captions for tables. Only one of them is given above. Writers are free to use any other style if they so prefer. What is important, however, is that the style used once should be consistently used all through the report.

The footnotes to the tables should be put immediately below the tables and not at the foot of the page as in the case of the footnotes to the text. To avoid confusion, it will be desirable to indicate the footnote mark in the table by symbols or small letters {*a, b, c,...z*}. Tables having more than two columns of facts should have their columns separated by vertical lines.

Illustrations: A research report may include graphs, pictures, plans, maps and diagrams as illustrative materials. Such illustrations should, as far as possible, follow their first reference in the text. Each illustration must have a caption and should be numbered in international numerals. As the illustrations form part of the text, they should be paginated consecutively with the textual matter (for the style of numbering illustrations, see the illustrations in this monograph).

Pagination

Every page of a report, including the blank ones, but excluding the blank sheet following the title page should be paginated. In the preliminaries the page numbers are indicated by small Roman numerals typed at the bottom of each page. The rest of the report should be numbered in international numerals centred at the top of the page. The page numbers can also be placed at the right hand corner of the page if so desired. A page, containing a major heading, i.e., chapter, will, however, bear its number only at the bottom of the page. Unless it is a small paper of informal nature, all major headings should be started on a new page.

Preparing Scientific Papers for Publication

In a small scientific paper prepared for a professional periodical, preliminaries are not important. In such cases, one should come immediately to the subject matter. It should, however, be divided into different sections. The whole paper should be typed in continuation putting the main and the sub-headings of various orders at their appropriate places.

References

Appendix

In the process of preparing a research report, a researcher may come across a lot of information which, although useful otherwise, will tend to detract the attention of the reader from the main theme of the paper if included in the text. This may include the details of the methodology used in the research process, lengthy tables giving facts and figures, derivation of mathematical formula, etc. Such materials can usefully be put in Appendices.

Each item of information should be kept in a separate appendix. The appendices may be numbered in capital letters or in capital Roman numerals.

Bibliography

Bibliography is the last important part of a research report. A bibliography lists the sources used in the preparation of the report. These may be:

1. Books;
2. Articles in periodicals;
3. Reports and documents issued by official or unofficial agencies;
4. Interviews;
5. Lectures, and
6. Radio and television talks.

If a bibliography is not a very long one, it can be put in alphabetical order by author. But if it is a long one and the references included are diverse, it should be classified according to types of publication. It can also be classified chapter-wise.

The forms of entries in the bibliography are different from that of the entries in the footnotes. Authors must keep this in mind. The usual forms are given below. These should be supplemented with the references given in the bibliography of this monograph and other publications.

> Chamberlin, T.C., and Salisbury, R.D., *Geology.* Vol. I: *Geologic Processes and Their Results.* 2nd ed. rev. New York: Henry Holt & Co., 1906.
>
> Hettner, Alfred. "Ferdinand von Richthofons Bedeutung fur die Geographic", *Geogr. Ztechr.*, 12 (1906), 1-11.
>
> Friedman, Milton. *Essays in Positive Economics.* Chicago: The University of Chicago Press, 1953.

If the bibliography is not an exhaustive one, the writer may call it "Select Bibliography", "Selected References" or "References Cited".

Index

If a research report is to be published, the writer may like to give an index at the end of the report. An index is given to assist readers to instantaneously spot the type of information they want to get. For example, a researcher may like to know whether there is any information in the report about the economic development of Africa. He can find it out easily if there is an index listing all important terms used (such as "Congo" and "Zambia") in the report in alphabetical order with the page numbers at which they appear in the text.

APPENDICES

Appendix - A
Samples of Table

Table 1: State-wise Distribution of Population in Arcadia, 1961.

Name of the State	*Population in Millions*
X	a
Y	b
Z	c
Total for Arcadia	a + b + c

Source: Arcadia Census Report. Part I, Vol. II, pp. 5-10.

Table 2: State-wise Distribution of Population in various Age Groups in Arcadia, 1961

Name of the State	*Population in millions*			
	Under 10 years	*10-20 years*	*20-50 years*	*Above 50 years*
1	2	3	4	5
X	—	—	—	—
Y	—	-	—	—
Z	—	—	—	—
Total	—	—	—	—

Source: Arcadia Census Report, Part I, Vol. III. pp. 100-120.

Note: It is absolutely necessary to give source of information used in the table.

Appendix - B
Abbreviations in Common Use

Singular	*Plural*	*Meaning*
2n ed.	—	second edition
art.	arts.	article (s)
Bk.	Bks.	Book(s)
cf	—	compare
chap.	chaps.	chapter (s)
col.	cols.	column (s)
ed.	eds.	editor (s)
et al.	—	and others
et passin	—	and here and there
Fig.	Figs.	figure (s)
ibid	—	(Latin *ibidem*) in the same place
Infra	—	below
Loc. cit.	—	(Latin loco citato) in the place cited
MS	MSS	manuscript (s)
N	nn	note
n.d.	—	no date
n.n.	—	no name
n.p.	—	no place
No.	Nos.	number (s)
oa.	—	about
op.cit.	—	(Latin opere citato) in the work cited
p.	pp.	page (s)
par.	pars.	paragraph (s)
passin.	—	here and there
pt.	pts.	part(s)
sec.	secs.	section (s)
supra.	—	above
trans.	—	translated by
vol.	vols.	volume (s)
vs.	vss.	verse (s)